READING
CHAMPS

OTHER WRITINGS BY RITA M. WIRTZ

Teaching for Achieving: How to Get the Achievement Results You Want. 1995.

K-3 Reading Success! Finding the Balance (What Works—How to Do It). 1996.

The Very Best Classroom-Tested Reading Strategies Ever! (Reading Success Recipes From 500 Classrooms). 1999.

Reading Champions! Master Training and Teaching Book. 2002.

Reading Champions! Teaching Reading Made Easy Video Set: Three Videos and Two Guidebooks. 2002.

"Creating Reading Champions!" (Newsletter article, CASCD), Foreword.

California Association for Supervision and Curriculum Development (CASCD), Vol. 15, No. 3. 2002.

California English-Language Arts Standards (Correlations with Reading Champions!). 2002.

For Teachers and Administrators (Helping Students Meet Reading Standards). 2003.

50 Common Sense Reading Lessons (Reading success recipes for teachers, parents, classroom assistants and home schooling families). 2003.

Corrective Reading: Word Study. Reading Champions! Teaching Reading Made Easy (Steffen's Story), Teaching a "Left Behind" Child to Read). 2005.

Guide Your Child Through
a World of Discovery

READING
CHAMPS

Teaching Reading Made Easy

RITA M. WIRTZ, MA

LifeRich Publishing books may be ordered through booksellers or by contacting:

LifeRich Publishing
1663 Liberty Drive
Bloomington, IN 47403
www.liferichpublishing.com
1 (888) 238-8637

ISBN: 978-1-4897-0208-1 (sc)
ISBN: 978-1-4897-0210-4 (hc)
ISBN: 978-1-4897-0209-8 (e)

Library of Congress Control Number: 2014909712

Printed in the United States of America.

LifeRich Publishing rev. date: 06/19/2014

ENDORSEMENTS

The development of Reading Champs spanned more than twenty-five years. Before it even started to become a book, it began as in-service programs for a few schools in a single district. The next step was the same programs provided for school district offices in their classrooms, which allowed Rita to demonstrate mini lesson practices in multiple environments. As the programs grew, more and more people sent letters and e-mails praising her work and the impacts teachers were seeing in their classrooms.

Here are just a few of the comments she received about Reading Champions.

"I have known Rita for over twenty years. I was one of her credential students at Chapman University in Sacramento, California, for my first teaching course. Later, as homeschool area coordinator in El Dorado County, I asked Rita to facilitate a workshop for teachers and parents in my program. She eagerly volunteered numerous times, instructing reading skills to homeschooled attendees. She also worked with parents and their children, grades K–12, at her home. Her newest literacy skills program works beautifully as a guide for teachers, parents, grandparents, and literacy instructors responsible for instructing children to read."

—Pam Laird, homeschool area coordinator, El Dorado County

"It is with pleasure that I write this letter for Rita Wirtz. I have known Rita for the past fifteen years. Her dedication and conscientious efforts teaching effective reading skills is demonstrated in her passion for learning and a commitment to high expectations for individual student performance.

Mrs. Wirtz has developed and designed multisensory and brain-based reading activities to teach critical reading, spelling, and writing skills. All these skills match the Common Core Standards. Mrs. Wirtz is a pioneer in project-based learning strategies and activities that teach mega-cognitive skills as the students advance in their reading fluency and comprehension. Her hands-on, multisensory, and collaborative teaching strategies model learning at its highest level. Reading Champs engages all learning styles!

Mrs. Wirtz is a diligent, lifelong learner with high expectations and ethical and core values that emanate from her resilience and energy in her professional development presentations and workshops on Reading Champs. Every reading program needs the foundational supports that Reading Champs brings to student success in reading fluency and comprehension!"

—Shirley Willadsen, MA, EdS, certified core adjunct professor, National University; Learning Resource Center director, Notre Dame Academy, San Diego, California

"Rita, who was my first public school principal, is still the most passionate educator I have encountered. Reading was always of prime importance on our campus, and she was leading the charge—reading to and with kids at every opportunity, even in the cafeteria and bus lines. She's a teacher's teacher who believes in every child's ability to learn. With her carefully crafted and tested lessons in this book, they will."

—Jeanette Kajka, master teacher, Robla School District, Sacramento, California

DEDICATION

Because kids don't come with instructions,
a little help goes a long way.

This book is dedicated to the children I taught in so many classrooms and the teachers I met along the way.

Special thanks to Steffen, Chase, Mackie, Kayla, Christian, Cameron, Hailey, Travis, Danielle, Jessica, and the many other children of all ages I taught at my mountain home. Each student became a confident, capable reader and writer after a very rough start in school. Most were in the bottom third, or lower, of their classes, failing and needing a big boost.

My gratitude to the principals, administrators, school board members, and parents who offered me teaching opportunities that made a huge difference to their students.

Of course, there is no way to thank my late husband, William, family, and friends, who supported me in every way all those years I was traveling the country looking for literacy answers.

To Margot Delfino, her husband, Jeff, Shirley Willadsen, Paula Weiss, Jeanette Kajka, Pam Laird, and Vicki Ludwig, you made a big difference to my work, and I am forever grateful.

Don and Estelle, where would this last project be without you? After my husband's lengthy illness and passing, thank you for encouraging me to finish this work, which I started in 2008.

Thank you to the three universities I taught for, the numerous organizations I presented for, the seminar companies who trusted me, and everyone who requested my keynotes.

San Diego County Office of Education, thank you for filming authentic (unrehearsed) classroom demonstration videos of my teaching.

California CASCD (California Association of Curriculum Development) for writing the book guide for my first *Reading Champions! Teaching Reading Made Easy* master book. I also appreciate Madera School District, correlating my work with state standards.

Bell Avenue school staff in Sacramento, being your principal was the best seven years of my life.

To all of you looking for answers, I am so proud to finally offer my life's work, the fundamentals of teaching reading, condensed into one jam-packed resource.

Warmly, Rita

EPIGRAPH

Never doubt that a small group of thoughtful, committed citizens
can change the world. Indeed, it's the only thing that ever has.

Margaret Mead (1901–1978)
Cultural anthropologist, researcher, and author

CONTENTS

LIST OF FIGURES

Full-size, full color, reproducible copies of all figures in this book are available through http://www.ritawirtz.com/supplies.

FOREWORD

I had been teaching for eighteen years in a small, high-poverty district in a school filled with troubled and sometimes forgotten children. Most of the dedicated teachers and staff were doing whatever they could to reach and teach, but we lived in the world of survival, not dreams. When Rita arrived as principal, she brought with her the vision and dreams that lifted our staff to new horizons. We came to believe that all children could learn and find a unique place in our school. They were valued and safe—and so were their families. We dug deeper into ourselves, found the strength to give even more, explored new child-centered programs, new curriculum and activities, and new ways to help children. Rita was the light.

She believed in us. Rita worked with struggling teachers so they could succeed and become master teachers themselves. Relationships with staff were not based on power; they were based on trust and shared goals. We would all succeed together.

Rita herself is a lifelong learner and educator. She taught reading at the K–12 levels and held several administrative positions. She was a university instructor, consultant, and trainer. As a reading coach, she provided in-classroom demonstrations and developed innovative approaches to meet the needs of challenging students. She was continuously refining her own understanding and techniques.

Her passion for teaching reading and her broad experiences have led her to develop several guides for reading instruction. This wonderful book, *Reading Champs*, is the culmination of Rita's life's work as she seeks to share her time-tested knowledge with you, your students, and your own children.

Reading Champs presents sets of concise, skilled mini lessons that focus on phonics instruction, structural analysis of language, and reading comprehension. It is meant to assist teachers and parents in helping children learn to read.

I have known Rita Wirtz for almost thirty years. She has inspired me, believed in me, and challenged my intellect. I love her, and you will too.

Paula H. Weiss, Title I teacher, retired

PREFACE

Why Do We All Need to Know This?

As parents, you can take the lead in ensuring that your child has the competitive edge, prepared to excel and compete for seats in the best colleges and universities or in any career path.

Concerned parents can and will play a major role in their children's success. It's a fact. Students are not reading any better despite increasing amounts of money poured into schools through federal programs such as No Child Left Behind. The most recent federal test scores from the National Assessment of Educational Progress (NAEP) revealed that only 35 percent of fourth graders and 36 percent of eighth graders are proficient readers. The US Department of Education and many states are currently mandating a common core curriculum.

This is just one of the reasons families are opting for alternative education environments. Because of the emphasis on preparing for high-stakes testing, children are not instructed in other important subjects. Home teaching, tutoring groups, peer-tutoring, charter schools, online schools, and innovative practices within traditional classroom environments are challenging teaching methods that have dominated the education community for more than a century.

Many children, some estimates as high as 50 percent, need additional assistance in mastering state standards and preparing for high-stakes standardized tests. This is true across the board, especially in the critical areas of literacy and reading, as evidenced by the NAEP scores.

Everyone teaching students to read has been looking for classroom-tested techniques to expand their inventory of tried-and-true methods and tools for their "teacher's toolbox."

The Reading Champs Common Sense Mini Lessons (CSML) program is intended to support—not replace—school curricula and reading programs. It provides a supplement for professional and nonprofessional "coaches," parents, tutors, classroom teaching assistants, and hardworking teachers. This "easy-start" how-to primer helps all students become better readers. It also helps connect the technical language of the school and classroom with real-life, at-home teaching and tutoring.

Reading Champs helps you know where to start and how to proceed with a structured, skill-based program. The wisest sages gave us the only real answer when they said, "Start at the very beginning."

This is the plan for Rita Wirtz' CSML instructional skill handbooks library. She starts at the beginning and moves upward. Following these easy-to-understand, step-by-step, research-proven reading activities for students and coaches to do together in one-hour units or chunks of twenty minutes or less makes teaching reading much easier.

However, and most important, this series empowers those working with frustrated, struggling, and often failing, readers. Teachers and teaching assistants find new ideas to fill learning gaps or validate and strengthen what is already working well.

To ensure that no child is left behind, it is important to foster a seamless, coordinated effort to reach and teach children at home as well as at school. Since parents are children's first and best teaching partners, well-informed parents and caregivers can assist with timely and appropriate intervention.

With all the educational stakeholders on the same page, teachers can share these mini lessons with families for helpful reinforcing lessons and extension activities for at-home tutoring. Individual instructional mini lessons are intended to assist Reading Champs coaches, and their students, in homeschool and other self-directed instructional programs in initial learning and unit review activities. Each title represents a single instructional unit, which is intended to

- encourage phonemic awareness and basic phonics (pk–K–1);
- teach decoding and word recognition (K–6);
- increase reading rate and fluency (K–6);
- build vocabulary, correct spelling, and concept development (K–12);
- read for meaning: structural features of texts/literature (K–12);
- build confidence based on comprehension;
- demonstrate that readers can become self-teachers in almost any subject; and
- create a "Recreational Reading" attitude.

About the Reading Champs CSML Coaches' Handbook

Use of graphics is limited intentionally to provide maximum information while keeping the number of pages and the cost of the materials lower for the user.

Each CSML section is a quick read for reading coaches, reducing lesson prep times and providing customized lessons to meet the needs of individual students. They are not intended to act as instructional readings for individual students. Although sample lesson plans are provided, the reading materials should be selected by the parent, coach, or tutor based on student interests and observed capabilities.

The library is presented as forty-nine topical sessions. Content and recommended sequencing of mini lessons is organized and aligned with the California State Board of Education Reading/Language Arts Framework, which was originally released in 1999 and revised in 2007. Additionally, because basic skills are universally accepted, the lessons align with most federal and state curricular frameworks and standards.

ACKNOWLEDGMENTS

Welcome to Reading Champs

Whether you are a parent helping a child learn to read, a reading specialist dealing with challenged readers, or an experienced teacher in almost any content area subject, these materials are written for you. There may be only one name on the cover of this book, but behind them are hundreds of others who have contributed greatly over the more than twenty years it has taken to create it. Parents, teachers, tutors, and even students provided invaluable insights and suggestions, leading to this final document.

These contributors are practitioners and administrators in public and charter school districts and classrooms, special needs instructors, linguistics researchers, homeschoolers, and college professors who have spent their careers teaching other teachers. Some are also teachers who were student teachers when they took Rita Wirtz' concepts and practices into their own classrooms and tutoring sessions to prove their validity.

Every teacher should be aware and know how to implement the time-tested information contained in the mini lessons. Understanding the how and why of any discipline cannot help but increase the competence of the practitioner. Much of the information presented here is taught in teacher-training courses but seldom in such a focused, concise, and comprehensive package.

The Key People behind Reading Champs

While there were hundreds of people who have played roles in the creation and preparation of this book, the following four individuals worked tirelessly in supporting Rita throughout the long journey from concept to completion.

William M. (Bill) Wirtz

Rita's husband of thirty-six years, Bill supported and encouraged Rita as Reading Champs grew from the seed of an idea to a small instructional outline and ultimately to where it is today.

Rita M. Wirtz, MA

Rita Wirtz earned a BA in English and speech and a master's in reading from Arizona State University (ASU) and an administrative services credential (K–12) through California State University–Sacramento (CSUS). Rita's classroom experience started with teaching grades seven to twelve English, speech, and reading lab. She went on to serve in administration as a K–6 and as a preschool principal. She also served as a Title I reading program evaluator and trainer at the state level and curriculum coordinator for the Sacramento County Office of Education. She continued training for a variety of seminar companies, numerous school districts and taught college reading courses for credential teachers and administrators. She has taught thousands of parents and caregivers, school board members, teachers, and administrators. Of most importance, Mrs. Wirtz demonstrated these mini lessons originally in nearly six hundred K–12 classrooms, including bilingual, special needs, and content area classes. Teachers followed her around her from class to class and recreated the lessons in their own classrooms. Because Rita walked the walk, she was highly regarded as a teachers' teacher.

Estelle S. Werve, MEd, MBA

Mrs. Werve is a social studies graduate of California State University–Sacramento (CSUS) and Chapman University in Sacramento, where she earned a secondary teaching credential with endorsements in ESL and multicultural education and a master's degree in curriculum and instruction. Estelle also served sixteen years as a member of the San Juan Unified School District, including three terms as board president, between 1990 and 2006. She was introduced to Reading Champs in 1991 when Rita was conducting a special seminar incorporated into the California School Board Association's (CSBA) Masters in Boardsmanship Academy (MBA). She immediately recognized the power and potential of the program.

Today, she continues working in the classroom as an on-call guest educator. She has been one of the key influences in the creation of this final series.

Donald E. Werve, Jr., MEd

Mr. Werve has enjoyed a long and diverse career as a professional writer, editor, and publisher in community journalism, general writing, and technical documentation. He is an English language arts graduate of California State University–Sacramento and Chapman University in Sacramento, where he earned a secondary teaching credential with endorsements in ESL and multicultural education, dual master's degrees in curriculum and instruction and leadership and administration, leading to a secondary administrative credential.

Don was introduced to Reading Champs by his wife, Estelle, after she attended a CSBA seminar where Rita was both a keynote speaker and presenter. Over the following twenty-two years, he has worked closely with Rita through more than a dozen changes, four revisions, and three fundamental reformats. His expertise in linguistics and language history provides a variety of interesting aspects for Reading Champs.

INTRODUCTION

Literacy and How to Pass It on to Others

We can tell you from experience that literacy, especially the ability to read, is the single most important skill that affects a student's ability to learn. Not all instructors understand the pedagogy (the science or profession of teaching) and practice of teaching reading. In many teacher-training courses and in-service training seminars, teachers are taught to use programs, not necessarily how to teach the skills themselves.

Learning to read is not just a mechanical process; it is also an emotional development. Reading Champs is designed to motivate students to want to learn and then to show them how to use the fundamental building blocks that are necessary for reading excellence. These success secrets work equally well for parents, tutors, and new or experienced teachers. They are powerful enough for classrooms and easy enough for use when teaching at home.

This introduction begins with something often not taught in college or in teacher-training classes and is the most important skill in any teacher's toolbox: the ability to motivate students to *want* to learn. Subject knowledge is secondary. If students are not motivated, the best teacher in the world is in trouble from day one.

In order to learn, students must be interested, have a need to know, and become engaged in the subject.

Teaching to a student's interests is a fact that has been well known for over 150 years, and more likely for more than a thousand years. Pioneer educator John Dewey said, "Teach the child where he is!" If a student is interested in art, demonstrate the ways the subject topic is related to art. If it is bicycles or cars, discover how art is related to mechanics; if it is mathematics, demonstrate the mathematics of perspective or the geometry of the Cubism, the school of art based geometric forms and structures.

The ideal instructional environment provides one-on-one teaching. This does not mean each student needs to have his or her own teacher all the time, but it does mean that each student gets individual attention in mini lessons. It is why small-group instruction, tutoring, or homeschooling succeeds—and a traditional classroom of twenty-five to thirty students falls short.

With one-on-one teaching, the student becomes the focus of the teacher's attention, and the teacher only needs to deal with one student's needs and personality.

Learning a Language Is Different from Any Other Subject

Language instruction techniques are more complex because each student moves from listening to speaking, then to reading, and finally to writing at his or her own pace. Competency in a language, or literacy, is a set of learned skills.

Many people believe primary speech occurs without instruction. For the most part, children learn language through a process called "total immersion." They learn their home language because it surrounds them daily in their environment. Its sounds, words, and meanings are part of the world around them. Reading is a far more intricate skill. It involves converting sounds to specific images (letters or numbers) and is learned through conscious efforts by teachers and students.

Starting as early as six months, babbling and pre-reading practice are encouraged. It does not require formal teaching skills, and most educators agree that parents are a child's first and most influential teachers. This is because the child learns by example. Parents who are consistent readers are more likely to raise successful readers than parents who don't read much. The Reading Champs project foundation is based on these widely recognized facts.

Reading Champs teaches students of any age how to read. The focus is *modeling, method,* and *pedagogy.* For the most part, it avoids specifying reading materials so instruction can flow with the interests of the student, guided by the teacher or tutor. This means the environment needs to have a wide variety of age-appropriate reading materials.

The Common Sense Reading Lesson (CSML) series consists of forty-nine handbooks that progressively cover different reading and writing skills.

Any student can become a reading champ! Similarly, almost anyone who knows how to read can be a reading coach. You don't need any special talent or kind of education. It only takes a personal love of reading and a dedication to helping others become successful.

Rita M. Wirtz, parent, educator, and author; creator of the Reading Champs series

Donald E. Werve Jr., M.Ed. parent, educator, writer, and editor

CSML-001: TEACHING AND LEARNING

Becoming an Effective Reading Champs Coach

Introduction: Things to Think About

Formal learning is a working partnership between a student and a teacher. When students are motivated and confident in their ability to learn, nothing can stop them. In addition, when they want or need to learn, and there is a desire, learning happens quickly. The information in this section helps anyone teaching students to read or to read better.

Let's start with the importance of using an easy-start way to consistently instruct. A typical Reading Champs guided reading lesson or mini lesson consists of a *Directed Reading Activity (DRA)*—an activity that develops or reviews a specific skill (refer to CSML-002 for more information about DRAs).

DRAs are generally used to teach word recognition or comprehension. When using a DRA, it is important the Reading Champs coach (reading teacher) uses a consistent lesson format.

Mini lessons should be planned to last from fifteen to twenty minutes, focusing on one concept at a time. At the end of each lesson, summarize what has been learned. If material is assigned for independent study, be sure to check that lesson for accuracy. Working with the student will be most effective. It is important to continually review (and reteach if necessary) materials within the planning stage for other lessons.

In this handbook, we deal with the details of planning and carrying out a Reading Champs instructional plan.

Almost every student, from preschooler through adult, has the potential to become a reading champion. But to make it happen, teaching practice has to follow the dictum of John Dewey, reaching and teaching students "where they're at" instead of where we think they should be.

We, every participant in the American education system, need to accept the fact that each student is unique. There is no such thing as a "standard" student. Only then will we be able to teach to each individual's needs, wants, and interests.

Who Are Reading Champs?

Reading Champs are high-achieving students, people of any age or gender, who have the power to enrich their lives because they are better able to read, understand, and make use of any kind of text, whether using a book, e-book, tablet, or computer. They aren't smarter than "average" people. They just seem smarter because they are usually better informed! They are easy to spot because:

Reading Champs read.

- They are usually more involved in the world around them.
- They know the stories behind the sound bites on the six o'clock news.
- They read to learn. More important, they know *how* to read to learn.
- They read faster than many people and retain more of what they read.
- They read for enjoyment. They build personal libraries of biographies, fiction, nonfiction, poetry, and textbooks, and they have access to online media.
- They are almost never bored.
- They would rather read than watch TV or play video games.

- They are usually better spellers and more interesting speakers.
- They often have higher self-esteem and are more self-confident.
- They are usually interesting because they are better conversationalists.
- They are often writers as well as readers.
- They enjoy greater job opportunities and are usually more capable at seeking out personally satisfying jobs.
- They are more likely to be promoted, even in tough economic times, because of their greater ability to communicate.

And almost anyone can be a Reading Champ because they are made—not born!

Even if you are not one yet, you can become a Reading Champ, and even a coach for future Reading Champs. You can help your children (or your students) become reading champs as well.

INSTRUCTIONAL ACTIVITY

Why Do We Need to Know This?

Most Reading Champs CSML plans start with this question because the question is often heard while students are learning to read and write (which we get into as we progress through the CSML handbooks). You will also notice that we try to use the word *we* whenever we talk about learning. We see learning as a partnership between an interested (motivated) student and a dedicated instructor. We begin the process by talking about how lessons should be conducted and why the information is presented as it is.

Practice

We assume that much of the material will be used by an experienced classroom teacher, reading coach, parent, or caregiver with an interest in helping the child or children become Reading Champs. For this reason, we use a consistent mini lesson planning format as much as possible. However, this same plan can be used to expand and master your own reading skills. Here's how to do it.

Coach: Provide a strong opener (or set) that briefly overviews the subject and outlines why it plays a necessary part in the overall learning process.

Coach/Student: Connect with prior knowledge. This is called schema or schemata. We believe all learning is based on and influenced by the student's knowledge and past experiences. This is critical!

Coach/Student: If continuing a cumulative lesson, for which related information has been presented previously, review the major points of the lesson(s). This provides an opportunity to refresh prior learning, if necessary.

Coach: Review the material being studied at intervals of eight to twelve seconds at first. As the student's memory span expands, review every thirty to forty-five seconds. Then review at appropriate, nonintrusive intervals during the lesson (every five to ten minutes). Finally, reinforce this by conducting reviews of previously-learned materials at the beginning of the next day, then one week, and again at one month and four months. (The one-month and four-month reviews can also be used as assessment reviews.)

Coach/Student: Introduce/investigate the new concept (letter, sound, words, phrases, sentences, or other material) in such a way that it ties into prior learning.

Coach/Student: Read a new text (paper, article, or story) that illustrates and reinforces the new concept.

Coach/Student: Find examples of the new concept in print, books of all sorts, and (where possible and appropriate) set up a print-rich environment or some other environment for "reading the room."

Coach/Student: Summarize what has been learned. If you are an independent learner, you will want to work with a mentor or a "study buddy" to verify and validate what you have learned.

Student: Strengthen the knowledge or skill with rehearsal, practice, memory drills (such as you will want to do with sight words), or playing games (Scrabble, for example, has different games for different skill levels.)

Student/Coach: Check for Understanding. (See "Informal Reading Inventories" in a later section of this series.)

Coach/Student: Develop a strong close to the lesson that summarizes the material covered in the mini lesson.

In the next three sections of this series, we start the learning process by demonstrating the concept of guided reading and the use of Directed Reading Activities (DRAs) as learning tools. They deal with the beginnings of phonemic awareness (and how to teach sounds) and gaining an understanding of letters as graphic representatives of sounds that are used to construct words, sentences, paragraphs, and a whole variety of texts.

READING CHAMPS LEARNING PLAN
Items shown in smaller type provides examples to assist you in preparation of each lesson.

UNIT TITLE: Example: **CSML-010: Consonants that Sound the Same**

RECOMMENDED MATERIALS:

Whenever possible, tactile and kinesthetic items should be incorporated into and used in instructional activities.

CSML-010 Handbook: Deck of Alphabet Cards (3"x 5" index cards 26 with upper case letters, 26 with lower case letters. These may be created in advance, or by the coach and student working together, or by the student copying the cards from a white board or word wall.)

Additional 3" x 5" index cards to continue development of sight reading cards containing both the letters and provided examples.

PREREQUISITES FOR LEARNING:

Per appropriate section in CSML-010 Handbook which can be tailored by the coach to fit student abilities and needs.

"WHY DO WE NEED TO KNOW THIS:"

Per appropriate section in CSML-010 Handbook which can be tailored by the coach to fit student abilities and needs.

LEARNING ACTIVITIES:

Information is provided in CSML-010 Handbook to which the coach may elect to add personal information. All examples should be modeled by the coach.

HELPFUL HINTS FOR LEARNERS:

Hints, mnemonics, and reinforcements to help students remember information either presented or reinforced by the material presented in the unit.

ADDITIONAL LEARNING OPPORTUNITIES:

Suggestions for more materials and resources that can be accessed by students to expand their knowledge base through independent studies. These may be additional materials provided as appendices to a learning unit or which might be readily available in local libraries, via Internet etc.

URLS FOR OTHER ASSOCIATED CSML UNITS, AS WELL AS APPROPRIATE EXTERNAL LINKS, MAY BE PROVIDED AS SUGGESTED TOPICAL CONTENT FOR STUDENTS ENGAGED IN INDEPENDENT STUDY.

SUMMARY:

The wrap-up of the learning unit. Reinforcement and extension activities. Motivate students to identify and pursue independent learning resources. Review and prepare for another upcoming teaching unit.

Figure 1-1: Lesson Planning Guide

READING CHAMPS LEARNING PLAN

Feel free to make copies of **this** page to help you in preparing lessons.

UNIT TITLE:
RECOMMENDED MATERIALS:
PREREQUISITES FOR LEARNING:
"WHY DO WE NEED TO KNOW THIS?"
LEARNING ACTIVITIES:
HELPFUL HINTS FOR LEARNERS:
ADDITIONAL LEARNING OPPORTUNITIES:
SUMMARY:

Figure 1-2: Lesson Planning Template

CSML-002: GUIDED READING

Easy-Start Directed Reading Activities (DRAs)

Introduction

This time-tested instructional guide is useful when you want to jumpstart an article, story chapter, or other text materials at the instructional level. You need an easy way to determine your student's instructional level if you don't know it yet. This means the student (beyond emergent) who reads a selection orally only misses one or two words out of twenty and has correct comprehension of three out of four questions.

By the end of the DRA, the student recognizes all words in the selection and understands the material completely. The Directed Reading Activity can be used for word study improvement or comprehension, alone or together.

Part 1

The Five Steps in a Traditional DRA*

1. Readiness
2. Guided silent reading
3. Discussion
4. "Independent" silent and/or oral reading

5. Follow-up, extension activities

Instructional Activity

Why Do We Have to Know This?

It is not unusual to hear the question while students are learning to read and write.

Most Reading Champs common sense mini lesson plans start with this question because students learn more quickly when there is a need to know something, an interest, and background knowledge to hook the new learning onto.

There are many ways lessons can be constructed, but the DRA provides a surefire reading success recipe to follow.

Practice

There are five steps in a traditional directed reading activity.*

1. Readiness: Ask yourself what you already know about the subject. Is there new vocabulary? The main purpose is to help develop interest in the subject.

Coaching Activities

- Introduce concepts and vocabulary needed to understand the selection. If appropriate, encourage your student to take notes.
- Working with your student, make a list of new words on a whiteboard or a piece of paper as they are introduced.
- Engage the student by providing reasons and asking questions to help him or her gain a purpose and interest in the material.

2. Guided Silent Reading: Read silently *and note unfamiliar words* before starting reading-aloud activities (except during diagnostic or assessment situations). Your goal is to boost comprehension of the overall text. This is best accomplished by asking specific word/content questions to establish the purpose for reading.

Coaching Activities

- Your student reads silently to find the answers to questions asked in Step 3 of the readiness activities. Questions might cover a single sentence, a question, a paragraph, a page, or an entire selection.

3. Discussion: Discuss the responses to questions (and answers) coming from the guided silent reading activities. These may lead to additional questions to stimulate interest, including facts (dates or people), inferences, conclusions, and vocabulary.

Coaching Activities

- Work with the vocabulary. Make sure all words (including phonic structures and correct spelling) are known.
- Ask additional questions to stimulate thinking.

4. Independent Silent or Oral Reading: In this activity, the student reads (or rereads) the selection silently or orally to find information to check the answers.

Coaching Activities

- Practice one or more word analysis (recognition) skill(s).
- Read a part (or parts) of the text to prove the answers given.
- Read larger parts just for fun (enjoy reading)!

5. Follow-up: Essentially, the follow-up step consists of activities and opportunities that lead to further understanding of the topic(s) studied. This includes appropriate extension activities.

Note to Coaches

Teaching a student "to read" is only half the job! Students improve their skills by independent practice and working on their own (or with a friend).

The DRA can also be used as a valuable diagnostic tool (refer to CSML-037): When you see your student "stuck" in particular activities, you know to review, reinforce, or reteach certain elements, words, or skills. The diagnostic-prescriptive-evaluative cycle tells the coach when to reteach or proceed.

Psychologist Hermann Ebbinghaus wrote that the greatest rate of forgetting takes place within twenty-four hours after something is heard or read, so always start your next lesson or mini lesson with a review. Even if your student appears to understand what you have just taught, always start with a review before teaching something new.

When teaching or reviewing a word analysis skill, choose whether to teach it in isolation or within the context of real reading (a working text). The best approach is to present the skill first and then practice both in and out of context. For example, if reviewing vowels, demonstrate the generalization first, find a corresponding example in a reading selection, and then practice the (new) skill in different ways until it is mastered.

When using the DRA for comprehension, the process is the same. That makes the DRA an extremely useful tool for teaching any mini lesson. In most lessons, word study and comprehension are taught together.

Part 2

Coach's Playbook
Instructional "Secrets"
Easy-Start Directed Reading Activity
Using a Content Area Textbook

Steps

1. Do a KWLW exercise first to find out what student(s) know. This should be fast! Check it out, and then start the skills. Relate all teaching to background experience, or build background experience as the connecting point.

2. Ask questions to clarify responses to the K (what I already know) and W (what I want to learn) portions of the KWLW process.

3. Introduce concepts and vocabulary necessary to understand the subject matter of the lesson.

4. Write new words on the board, chart, or one of the vocabulary formats.

5. Make sure to motivate students about the subject and get their attention.

6. Direct silent reading. Have a purpose for the reading. Use formats to do the predictions.

7. Ask question(s) to guide the reading. Use Mrs. Words (Rita Wirtz') "Four Big Ideas" or other means of organizing students' thinking during the silent reading.

8. You may want to do a book, chapter or article walk.

9. Tell students to find the answer or answers to your questions. These may be based on a sentence, paragraph, or page.

10. Discuss the students' responses. Were their predictions accurate?

11. Clear up any vocabulary confusion or comprehension mistakes.

12. Oral reading or rereading of critical portions of the text.

Then drill and practice to review all basic skills to ensure memory.

When you teach skills in isolation ("detached" as Monday, review one thing on Tuesday, etc.) be sure to put everything back together so students are not stuck with unconnected pieces of learning.

If students appear to have mastered something, fine, but don't assume it is really, totally, learned. Remember the Ebbinghaus curve of forgetting shows most information heard once or twice is forgotten within twenty-four hours. A cycle of review, repeat, and apply is a great way to teach (or reteach) fundamental skills.

Part 3

Structuring a CSML

A typical mini lesson (fifteen- or twenty-minute chunks) might consist of the following activities:

- word recognition skills review
- developing basic subject matter concepts
- expanding vocabulary
- practicing reading comprehension strategies

Select the particular activities appropriate to lesson time frame and students' instructional needs.

The basic goal for the Easy-Start DRA should be that students recognize all the words they are reading, with complete understanding of the content as well. Obviously, the reading lesson should be at an instructional, rather than a frustration, level. Be sure to model everything you want students to know and do before they are expected to repeat the strategies without help.

Practice perfects performance! (Practice makes permanent!)

Part 4

Shortcuts
How to Improve Comprehension

First of all, what should students know? What do they need to know to master the content? This determines what you should be teaching. In addition to the content, here are comprehension skills to focus on (until mastery):

1. Making predictions and having a purpose to read. Develop questions to look for.

2. Following directions (the linear way of doing things correctly, listening, and "attending" to the task).
3. Recognizing the main idea or the key big idea(s) of the selection.
4. Noting the details (factual data, including details that explain, clarify, further illustrate, or describe).
5. Organizing the ideas (Seeing relationships among the ideas, grouping by attributes).
6. Determining the sequence (the order of steps in a process, event, etc.).
7. Knowing the meanings of words. A reader's vocabulary is dependent upon background experience and level of information about the subject. Wide reading builds a stronger vocabulary.

Organize your own thoughts and ideas!

CSML-003: TEACHING SOUNDS

(Phonemic Awareness)

Introduction

New readers manipulate speech sounds before they learn letters and letter-sound relationships (phonics). Budding readers of any age appreciate wordplay of varied types, helping them focus on sounds and developing an awareness of different sounds in words. This is true for the baby learning to articulate sounds (which can begin as "baby babble" at as early as two months) or for the individual of any age learning English as a second language.[1]

Reading Champs mini lessons offer experiences in rhythm and rhyme, segmenting (syllabication) and synthesis, sound sequence, isolation, substitution, and blending (see below). These interesting patterns are used in many well-known books featuring rhythm, rhyme, repetition, and

---

1   One of the most difficult components of English to learn for ESL students is the number and complexity of vowel sounds. Most languages based on the Greek alphabet have clearly defined phonic identity. Using Spanish, as an example, the letter *A* has a single sound (ah). However, in English we find anywhere from four to seven sounds. Because the ability to read and understand is closely tied to hearing with understanding, the first step to bilingual instruction should always be to understand the differences between the two languages.

predictable patterns. Classic nursery rhymes are wonderful and certainly have stood the test of time.

Reading coaches should gather pictures, photo and letter cards, cubes, tiles, games, and a variety of music that features various kinds of rhythms for their teaching toolbox. Instruments, especially drums (bongos, congas, or pencil erasers on the bottom of an empty tin can) are fun to use for accompaniment and feel the beat.

Teachers disagree about whether phonemic awareness can or should be taught as a reading skill. Opponents state that language learning is a natural process.[2] At the other extreme are educators who believe in testing progress learning the various skills. It makes sense to offer many opportunities that focus on individual elements of phonemic awareness through a series of mini lessons.

Why Do We Need to Know This?

Reading experts agree that phonemic awareness is a predictor for reading success. At-home teachers and tutors (Reading Champs coaches) and classroom teachers need to spend plenty of time on wordplay. Have fun reading aloud, singing, chanting, and playing with the sounds of the language in a variety of ways.

Phonics Vocabulary

Isolation: Identifying individual sounds as in words such as *pin: p-i-n, bin: b-i-n, din: d-i-n (which means a lot of noise), fin: f-i-n,* or *tin: t-i-n.*

Sequence: Identifying the order sounds are heard in the word at the beginning, in the middle, or at the end of the word.

Substitution: Practicing the effect of changing sounds, such as *bat, cat, fat, and hat.*

Blending: Combining individual letter sounds into words: / m / a / n / to *man.*

---

2   Language learning *is* a natural process as verbal language is acquired from environment. Reading (also referred to as decoding), however, is an instructed (show and tell) skill.

Instructional Activities and Games

Coach-Directed Activities

See and Say

"What sound *(not what letter)* does your name start with?" or "What is another word that begins with this sound?" or hold up a sight-word flash card and ask, "What is the first sound in this word?"

For example, the first letter in *Bob* would be *buh.*

Hear and Move

"Nod your head, clap your hands, and wiggle your hips, etc., when you hear the first, middle, and last sound in this word." Take a list of ten words and ask, "Which of these words begins with the same sound?" "What rhymes with house?"

Say, "Tap your foot when you hear the sound in the middle" (use a group of three-phoneme words for this one). "Find the letter that makes this sound." "Tap your pencil when you hear a different sound." "Which sound comes last in this word?"

Look, Listen, and Feel

Place a tissue in front of your mouth, and then when you model sounds, see which sounds move the tissue most (probably the *p*, followed closely by the sound for *th* and the sound for *sh*. Put your fingers on your throat and feel different sounds (voiced and unvoiced, as this or think, very different).

Rhyme or No Rhyme

Make yes and no index cards. Green for yes and red for no. Use construction paper or sturdier cardboard with a happy face and a sad face for younger children. Slates or whiteboards are great. When two rhyming words are heard, hold up the yes card; if the words don't rhyme, show the no card.

How Many Sounds Do You Hear?

"Use your fingers to show how many sounds you hear in this word."

Twitch the Tail: Heads and Tails

Use string or bendable wax play sticks to put a head or tail on a drawing of a cat or dog. Use this to represent the sound at the beginning or end of a word. When the coach holds up a word or makes a sound, the student moves the head or moves the tail.

A Stitch in Time ...

Have an enjoyable time reading aloud, doing nursery rhymes, tongue twisters, easy songs, and chants. Remember that the purpose of these lessons is to learn early phonic and word skills.

Summary

Reading experts generally agree that phonemic awareness is one of the early predictors for reading success. It is appropriate for classroom teachers (at school) and at-home teachers, parents, and tutors (Reading Champs coaches) to spend a lot of time on wordplay. Read aloud and play with the sounds of the language. Older students might enjoy seeing the classic movie *My Fair Lady* with Audrey Hepburn and Rex Harrison.

CSML-004: THE ALPHABET LANGUAGE SKILL

Teaching and Learning Letters

Introduction

Welcome to the world of the alphabet, a rich, easy-to-understand set of rules that kick off the Reading Champs instructional handbooks. These simple, Easy-Start reading success secrets make a big difference in your teaching and coaching!

Before we start with the alphabet, you need to know a few things. First, each letter represents one or more sounds, and second, all printed and written words have meaning.

All English text is made up of letters and combinations of letters called words; each word is separated from every other word by one or more spaces and, in some cases, symbols known as punctuation.

The next fact is that English is read from left to right and from the upper-left corner of the text to the bottom-right corner.

And, finally, the letters of the alphabet are presented in UPPERCASE LETTERS and lowercase letters. It is important that English-language learners are aware of these differences and the rules that govern their use.

Why Do We Need to Know This?

Few elements of the English language are as important as our alphabet. Using only twenty-six symbols, we can construct tens of thousands of different words. We describe those words later in these instructional handbooks, but before we do, you need to understand what these symbols are and how they are used to represent sounds.

We believe the English alphabet is the most important of all the elements that define our language. Here's what you need to know to jumpstart your teaching.

Instructional Activities

Introduction to the Alphabet

Just like people, some letters are short, and some are tall; some are sort of thin, some are medium sized, and some are wide. Some letters have tails, and some have lines moving through them. Some letters are doubled up in words, and others never stand together. But they are all symbols for sounds, and those sounds make syllables, words, and sentences.

How to Recognize Letters in the Alphabet

There are four lowercase letters with tails: *y, p, q,* and *j.*

There are four lowercase letters with sticks: *p, b, l,* and *m.*

There are four lowercase letters with circles: *o, a, d,* and *p.*

There are three lowercase letters with tunnels: *h, m,* and *n.*

There are three tall lowercase letters: *f, h,* and *l.*

There are four short lowercase letters: *a, c, n,* and *u.* (or *c u a n*) if you really want to remember them that way).

There are three lowercase letters with crossing lines: *f, t,* and *x.*

There are two lowercase letters with dots: *i* and *j.*

There are four curving lowercase letters: *m, n, e,* and *f.*

There are two slanting lowercase letters: *x* and *y.*

And there are three letters whose lowercase and uppercase look about the same:

Ss, Xx, and *Yy.*
All the *uppercase* letters are about the same size:
A, B, C, D, E, F, G, H, I, J, K, L, M,
N, O, P, Q, R, S, T, U, V, W, X, Y, and Z.
All the *lowercase* letters are different sizes and shapes:
a, b, c, d, e, f, g, h, i, j, k, l, m,
n, o, p, q, r, s, t, u, v, w, x, y, and *z.*

What are the letters in your first name? You may print them in all uppercase letters.

The Word Wall Card (see next page) is designed so students can rearrange them easily into small packets to demonstrate an understanding of the concepts described above.

Example: This word wall card layout is intended for a 4" x 6" index card. Letters are presented in both uppercase and lowercase letters and in Times New Roman *(a serif face) and* Arial *(a sans-serif face). Four words are provided so the student can find, cut, and paste illustrations of each of the example words. Complete sets as .pdf files are available at ritawirtz.com. Feel free to use this idea to create your own set.*

*Example: This Word wall Card layout is intended for a 4" x 6" index card. Letters are presented in both upper and lower case letters and in **Times New Roman** (a serif face) and **Arial** (a sans-serif face). Four words are provided so the student can find, cut, and paste illustrations of each of the example words. Complete, sets of 26 full-sized full-color sheets are available from <u>supplies@ ritawirtz.com</u> but you can use this idea to create your own set.*

WORD WALL ALPHABET CARD

apple   astronaut

A a

A a

airplane   automobile

The letter *"a"* is a vowel

Figure 4-1: Word Wall Alphabet Card

(Appropriate illustrations might be provided as examples for paste-ons.)

CSML-005: RECOGNIZING SIGHT WORDS

Introduction

Part 1

Beginning and emerging readers look for letters and words everywhere—in names, on street signs, labels, cereal boxes (where they also find graphic clues), etc. Use experience, environmental print, and word lists to teach sight words. Students realize there are plenty of opportunities to find these words in a variety of places or contexts.

Students need to start with the easiest words first. It is helpful to begin with concrete objects from around the house or classroom since most sight word lists are full of abstract words challenging for the beginning and emerging reader. (*For example, what is a "the"?*) One of the best things to start with is the student's own name.

In creating your word lists—items for a print-rich environment and word wall—be sure to include the basic sight words, which are said to make up 50 percent of all reading materials. See our Easy-Start sight word lists.

Why Do We Need to Know This?

Part 2

Drill and repetition help emerging readers remember new, unknown words whenever they see them. Since sight words are first recognized by shape, begin using configuration cues (shape cues, as in the word *monkey*) rather than reading one letter at a time. When drilling words, place the known words at the back of the pack. Keep reviewing all the words, but focus on the words missed.

Singing, chanting, and word games can be useful. Another time-tested technique is to put new words on shower curtain rings, flash cards, or in a recipe file box.

Remember, the skill is to be able to read a word and to quickly recognize what that word means so your student can keep on *moving*.

Instructional Activity

Instructional Practice

Part 3

Create opportunities on a daily basis to engage in listening, speaking, reading, and writing. Creating a word wall with sight words written on a large sheet of poster board, butcher paper, or individual index cards reinforces sight words. Color-coded word strips with key pictures can easily be created.

a	at	and	as	all	am	always	an	are	again
about	anything	by	be	big	because	but	been	can	come
could	do	did	does	down	eat	each	enough	early	easy
even	every	everyone	enough	for	far	from	first	go	get
had	her	have	how	has	he	him	help	I	it
in	is	if	its	just	let	like	look	my	more
maybe	me	most	many	make	most	no	not	now	nothing
or	of	on	off	once	over	out	one	often	other
probably	please	play	put	quiet	quite	run	read	red	ran
ready	real	sit	say	she	see	so	some	said	should
something	sometimes	to	the	they	then	that	this	today	there
through	their	these	then	to	two	too	up	under	use
very	was	will	we	way	who	word	would	with	were
which	what	when	while	where					

Figure 5-1: Easy-Start Sight List

Since it is important for students to recognize sight words, start with this Easy-Start list or the well-known *The Reading Teacher's Book of Lists* is also a great, respected resource.

Some researchers say learning a sight word is sheer repetition; it takes four to fifteen exposures to remember a new word. Obviously, there are other emotional and environmental factors. Learners, especially young children, emergent readers, and ELL (second language learners) quickly remember new words.

Part 4

Check this out!

Instructional Practice (Sight Words)

Abbreviations Commonly Used in Print

a.m. (morning); p.m. (afternoon, evening); p. or pg. (page); pp. (pages); etc. (etcetera; and so on); MD (medical doctor); lb. (pound); c/o (in care of); Mr. (mister); Ms. (miss or missus); Mrs. (missus) PS (postscript); mph (miles per hour); mpg (miles per gallon); Ave. (avenue); US and USA (United States and United States of America) and more.

Note: Common practice allows abbreviations to be written without the periods, but their usage is still seen as correct usage. Other common information that is often abbreviated includes:

- days of the week
- months of the year
- states
- measurements
- names (and nicknames) such as J. P. (John Pelham)

Other common words include the names of numbers, letters, shapes, and the seven principal colors—red, orange, yellow, green, blue, indigo, and violet—the colors of a rainbow.

Instructional Practice

Part 5: Tactile-Kinesthetic Exercises

Instructional Aids for Learners with Alternate Learning Styles

Words, especially sight words and abbreviations (above), can be drilled by using tracing techniques, games, and other activities that appeal to the senses. Say a word, then write it out, act it out, manipulate it, and look for the word on the word wall. Letters and words can also be built by using library paste and salt or sand. A long-term activity could build tiles (using ceramic or vinyl tiles or even artists' clay) of the twenty-six letters and ten numbers (*remember that zero is a number*).

Part 6

This list, and those on the following pages, contains three hundred of the words considered most important sight reading words.

To assist with visual recognition, the lists are also provided in Times New Roman and Arial/Helvetica); the two types faces used most commonly in books and publications.

FIRST 100 LIST (Times New Roman)

(Grade level indicated in parentheses following the word in these tables are those identified as appropriate words for writing grade level texts.)

(k) = kindergarten; (1) = first grade; (2) = second grade, etc.

a *(k)*	about *(k)*	after *(k)*	again *(k)*	all *(k)*	an *(k)*
and *(k)*	any *(k)*	are *(k)*	as *(k)*	at *(k)*	be *(k)*
before *(k)*	boy *(k)*	but *(k)*	buy *(k)*	can *(k)*	come *(k)*
day *(k)*	did *(k)*	do *(k)*	down *(k)*	eat *(k)*	for *(k)*
from *(k)*	get *(k)*	give *(k)*	go *(k)*	good *(k)*	had *(k)*
has *(k)*	have *(k)*	he *(k)*	her *(k)*	here *(k)*	him *(k)*
his *(k)*	how *(k)*	I *(k)*	if *(k)*	in *(k)*	is *(k)*
it *(k)*	just *(1)*	know *(1)*	like *(k)*	little *(k)*	long *(1)*
make *(k)*	man *(k)*	many *(k)*	me *(k)*	much *(1)*	my *(k)*
new *(k)*	no *(k)*	not *(k)*	of *(k)*	old *(k)*	on *(k)*
one *(k)*	or *(k)*	other *(1)*	our *(k)*	out *(k)*	put *(k)*
said *(k)*	see *(k)*	she *(k)*	so *(k)*	some *(k)*	take *(k)*
that *(k)*	the *(k)*	their *(k)*	them *(k)*	then *(k)*	there *(1)*
they *(k)*	this *(k)*	three *(k)*	to *(k)*	two *(k)*	up *(k)*
us *(k)*	very *(k)*	was *(k)*	we *(k)*	were *(k)*	what *(k)*
when *(k)*	which *(1)*	who *(k)*	will *(k)*	with *(k)*	work *(k)*
wolf *(1)*	would *(1)*	you *(k)*	your *(k)*		

Figure 5-2: Easy-Start Sight List (1)

SECOND 100 LIST (Times New Roman)

(Grade level indicated in parentheses following the word in these tables are those identified as appropriate words for writing grade level texts.)

(k) = kindergarten; (1) = first grade; (2) = second grade, etc.

also *(k)*	am *(k)*	another *(1)*	away *(k)*	back *(k)*	ball *(k)*
because *(k)*	best *(k)*	better *(k)*	big *(k)*	black *(k)*	book *(k)*
both *(k)*	box *(k)*	bring *(k)*	call *(k)*	came *(k)*	color *(k)*
could *(k)*	dear *(1)*	each	ear *(1)*	end *(k)*	far *(1)*
find *(k)*	first *(k)*	five *(k)*	found *(k)*	four *(k)*	friend *(1)*
girl *(k)*	got *(k)*	hand *(k)*	high *(k)*	home *(k)*	house *(k)*
into *(1)*	kind *(k)*	last *(k)*	leave *(1)*	left *(1)*	let *(k)*
live *(1)*	look *(k)*	made *(k)*	may *(k)*	men *(1)*	more *(k)*
morning *(1)*	most *(1)*	mother *(k)*	must *(1)*	name *(k)*	near *(1)*
never *(k)*	next *(k)*	night *(1)*	only *(k)*	open *(k)*	over *(k)*
own *(1)*	people *(k)*	play *(k)*	please *(k)*	present *(k)*	pretty *(k)*
ran *(k)*	read *(k)*	red *(k)*	right *(k)*	run *(k)*	saw *(k)*
say *(k)*	school *(k)*	seem *(1)*	shall *(1)*	should *(1)*	soon *(k)*
stand *(k)*	such *(1)*	sure *(k)*	tell *(k)*	than *(k)*	these *(k)*
thing *(k)*	think *(1)*	too *(1)*	tree *(k)*	under *(k)*	until *(1)*
upon *(1)*	use *(k)*	want *(k)*	way *(k)*	where *(1)*	while *(1)*
white *(k)*	why *(k)*	wish *(k)*	year *(1)*		

Figure 5-3: Easy-Start Sight List (2)

THIRD 100 LIST (Times New Roman)

(Grade level indicated in parentheses following the word in these tables are those identified as appropriate words for writing grade level texts.)

(k) = kindergarten; (1) = first grade; (2) = second grade, etc.

along *(1)*	always *(k)*	anything *(1)*	around *(1)*	ask *(k)*	ate *(k)*
bed *(k)*	brown *(k)*	buy *(k)*	car *(k)*	carry *(k)*	clean *(k)*
close *(k)*	clothes *(1)*	coat *(1)*	cold *(k)*	cut *(k)*	didn't *(1)*
does *(1)*	dog *(k)*	don't *(1)*	door *(k)*	dress *(k)*	early *(1)*
eight *(1)*	every *(k)*	eye(s) *(k)*	face *(k)*	fall *(k)*	fast *(1)*
fat *(1)*	fine *(1)*	fire *(k)*	fly *(k)*	food *(k)*	full *(k)*
funny *(1)*	gave *(k)*	goes *(1)*	green *(k)*	grow *(k)*	hat *(k)*
happy *(k)*	hard *(k)*	head *(k)*	hear *(k)*	help *(k)*	hold *(1)*
hope *(k)*	hot *(k)*	jump *(k)*	keep *(k)*	letter *(1)*	longer
love *(k)*	might *(1)*	money *(k)*	myself *(1)*	now *(k)*	o'clock *(4)*
off *(k)*	once *(1)*	order *(1)*	pair *(1)*	part *(1)*	ride *(k)*
round *(k)*	same *(k)*	sat	second *(1)*	set *(k)*	seven *(k)*
show *(1)*	sing *(1)*	sister *(1)*	sit *(k)*	six *(k)*	sleep *(k)*
small *(k)*	start *(1)*	stop *(k)*	ten *(k)*	thank *(1)*	third *(1)*
those *(1)*	though *(1)*	today *(k)*	took *(1)*	town *(k)*	try *(k)*
turn *(1)*	walk *(k)*	warm *(1)*	wash *(1)*	water *(k)*	woman *(k)*
write *(k)*	yellow *(k)*	yes *(k)*	yesterday *(3)*		

Figure 5-4: Easy-Start Sight List (3)

FIRST 100 LIST (Arial / Helvetica)

(Grade level indicated in parentheses following the word on these tables are those identified as appropriate words for writing grade level texts.)

(k) = kindergarten; (1) = first grade; (2) = second grade, etc.

a *(k)*	about *(k)*	after *(k)*	again *(k)*	all *(k)*	an *(k)*
and *(k)*	any *(k)*	are *(k)*	as *(k)*	at *(k)*	be *(k)*
before *(k)*	boy *(k)*	but *(k)*	buy *(k)*	can *(k)*	come *(k)*
day *(k)*	did (k)	do *(k)*	down *(k)*	eat *(k)*	for *(k)*
from *(k)*	get *(k)*	give *(k)*	go *(k)*	good *(k)*	had *(k)*
has *(k)*	have *(k)*	he *(k)*	her *(k)*	here *(k)*	him (k)
his *(k)*	how *(k)*	I *(k)*	if *(k)*	in *(k)*	is *(k)*
it *(k)*	just *(1)*	know *(1)*	like *(k)*	little *(k)*	long *(1)*
make *(k)*	man *(k)*	many *(k)*	me *(k)*	much *(1)*	my *(k)*
new *(k)*	no *(k)*	not *(k)*	of *(k)*	old *(k)*	on *(k)*
one *(k)*	or *(k)*	other *(1)*	our *(k)*	out *(k)*	put *(k)*
said *(k)*	see *(k)*	she *(k)*	so *(k)*	some *(k)*	take *(k)*
that *(k)*	the *(k)*	their *(k)*	them *(k)*	then *(k)*	there *(1)*
they *(k)*	this *(k)*	three *(k)*	to *(k)*	two *(k)*	up *(k)*
us *(k)*	very *(k)*	was *(k)*	we *(k)*	were *(k)*	what *(k)*
when *(k)*	which *(1)*	who *(k)*	will *(k)*	with *(k)*	work *(k)*
wolf *(1)*	would *(1)*	you *(k)*	your *(k)*		

Figure 5-5: Easy-Start Sight List (4)

SECOND 100 LIST (Arial / Helvetica)

(Grade level indicated in parentheses following the word are those identified as appropriate words for writing grade level texts.)

(k) = kindergarten; (1) = first grade; (2) = second grade, etc.

also *(k)*	am *(k)*	another *(1)*	away *(k)*	back *(k)*	ball *(k)*
because *(k)*	best *(k)*	better *(k)*	big *(k)*	black *(k)*	book *(k)*
both *(k)*	box *(k)*	bring *(k)*	call *(k)*	came *(k)*	color *(k)*
could *(k)*	dear *(1)*	each	ear *(1)*	end *(k)*	far *(1)*
find *(k)*	first *(k)*	five *(k)*	found *(k)*	four *(k)*	friend *(1)*
girl *(k)*	got *(k)*	hand *(k)*	high *(k)*	home *(k)*	house *(k)*
into *(1)*	kind *(k)*	last *(k)*	leave *(1)*	left *(1)*	let *(k)*
live *(1)*	look *(k)*	made *(k)*	may *(k)*	men *(1)*	more *(k)*
morning *(1)*	most *(1)*	mother *(k)*	must *(1)*	name *(k)*	near *(1)*
never *(k)*	next *(k)*	night *(1)*	only *(k)*	open *(k)*	over *(k)*
own *(1)*	people *(k)*	play *(k)*	please *(k)*	present *(k)*	pretty *(k)*
ran *(k)*	read *(k)*	red *(k)*	right *(k)*	run *(k)*	saw *(k)*
say *(k)*	school *(k)*	seem *(1)*	shall *(1)*	should *(1)*	soon *(k)*
stand *(k)*	such *(1)*	sure *(k)*	tell *(k)*	than *(k)*	these *(k)*
thing *(k)*	think *(1)*	too *(1)*	tree *(k)*	under *(k)*	until *(1)*
upon *(1)*	use *(k)*	want *(k)*	way *(k)*	where *(1)*	while *(1)*
white *(k)*	why *(k)*	wish *(k)*	year *(1)*		

Figure 5-6: Easy-Start Sight List (5)

THIRD 100 LIST (Arial / Helvetica)

(Grade level indicated in parentheses following the word in these tables are those identified as appropriate words for writing grade level texts.)

(k) = kindergarten; (1) = first grade; (2) = second grade, etc.

along *(1)*	always *(k)*	anything *(1)*	around *(1)*	ask *(k)*	ate *(k)*
bed *(k)*	brown *(k)*	buy *(k)*	car *(k)*	carry *(k)*	clean *(k)*
close *(k)*	clothes *(1)*	coat *(1)*	cold *(k)*	cut *(k)*	didn't *(1)*
does *(1)*	dog *(k)*	don't *(1)*	door *(k)*	dress *(k)*	early *(1)*
eight *(1)*	every *(k)*	eye(s) *(k)*	face *(k)*	fall *(k)*	fast *(1)*
fat *(1)*	fine *(1)*	fire *(k)*	fly *(k)*	food *(k)*	full *(k)*
funny *(1)*	gave *(k)*	goes *(1)*	green *(k)*	grow *(k)*	hat *(k)*
happy *(k)*	hard *(k)*	head *(k)*	hear *(k)*	help *(k)*	hold *(1)*
hope *(k)*	hot *(k)*	jump *(k)*	keep *(k)*	letter *(1)*	longer
love *(k)*	might *(1)*	money *(k)*	myself *(1)*	now *(k)*	o'clock (4)
off *(k)*	once *(1)*	order *(1)*	pair *(1)*	part *(1)*	ride *(k)*
round *(k)*	same *(k)*	sat	second *(1)*	set *(k)*	seven *(k)*
show *(1)*	sing *(1)*	sister *(1)*	sit *(k)*	six *(k)*	sleep *(k)*
small *(k)*	start *(1)*	stop *(k)*	ten *(k)*	thank *(1)*	third *(1)*
those *(1)*	though *(1)*	today *(k)*	took *(1)*	town *(k)*	try *(k)*
turn *(1)*	walk *(k)*	warm *(1)*	wash *(1)*	water *(k)*	woman *(k)*
write *(k)*	yellow *(k)*	yes *(k)*	yesterday *(3)*		

Figure 5-7: Easy-Start Sight List (6)

CSML-006: THE CUEING PROCESS

Word Study for Reading Comprehension

Introduction

Readers use a combination of three or more systems to make meaning of print. Each approach is used simultaneously, at least to some degree.

1. *Semantics:* The meaning of the word or phrase.
2. *Syntactics:* The structure of the word or phrase.
3. *Graphophonics:* Print and sound symbol correspondence.

David Booth says, "Reading is an interactive process in which the reader uses a variety of strategies for comprehension."

Why Do We Need to Know This?

Cueing is an important strategy to learn. It offers an opportunity to quickly recognize unknown words or phrases and helps make sense of print.

Instructional Activity

Offer opportunities to help students anticipate the meaning of print as well as language patterns and phonic cues. These clues include semantic, syntactic normalcy (essentially the "comfort" of the listener's or reader's language experience), and graphophonic. In each case, recognizing linguistic convention takes the form of a question.

- **Semantic:** "Does this make sense? Look at the picture again. Reread the sentence."
- **Syntactic:** "Does this sound right to you? Can you say it another way? What other word (or phrase) might fit here?"
- **Graphophonic:** "Does this look right to you? What letter or sound does it begin with? Point to the letter (or word)." Or ask, "Does this look familiar? Take another look at this. What does this letter (or word) look like? Look for a little (smaller) word inside this word. Check this word with one you already know."

Note to Coaches

Practice each type of strategy in various written materials. Start with easy text and progress to more difficult (and challenging) reading materials. Cueing can provide extremely valuable skills if they are reviewed and practiced at each progressive learning level and across every level of content.

CSML-007: EASY-START DIAGNOSTIC INVENTORY

Systematic Phonics Sequence 1

Teaching Word Recognition

Introduction

Second language learners, ESL students, and ELL students find it difficult to transfer many sounds to English. In most non-English languages, vowels only have one sound; some consonants don't make the same sound. For instance, *v* might sound like *b*, *ch* like *sh*, *ll* like *y*, etc.

Diagnostic data from formal or informal assessment is important, whether for primary English learners or second language students. Without this, it is difficult to know which elements of the systematic phonics sequence to teach or reteach. If you don't have this information already, look at the Easy-Start Diagnostic Inventory and Informal Reading Inventory elsewhere in this series.

For example, does your student know basic sight words? What skills does he have for sounding out unknown words? Does he know short vowel sounds? Does she know long vowel sounds? Can he blend letters and sounds easily to form words (for example s-a-t to *sat*? Can she read consonant blends (such as *st* or *br*)?

Are consonant combinations or diagraphs *ch, sh, th,* and *wh* known? Can he recognize vowel combinations, such as *oa, ai, ou,* and *ow*? Can she read and properly pronounce vowels followed by *r,* such as *ar, er, ir, or,* and *ur*?

Why Do We Need to Know This?

Learning to read is like building a brick wall. You start with a foundation made up of past knowledge and experiences. Then you select bricks that make the wall you want.

In language, these bricks are different letters, and every one of these bricks has its own sound. In this instructional unit, you learn to be a word detective, with reading success recipes and secrets for mastering the systematic phonics sequence.

In the next eleven sections, mini lessons focus on special characteristics of each fundamental building block.

Instructional Activity

Guided Instruction

Determine if the student can discriminate between similar sounds like *lap* and *lack* or *some* and *son* or *sun.*

Using the following mini lessons (CSML-008 through SML-019), teach one sound, letter, or pattern each day for the first time. Start by reviewing, and then fill in the gaps and correct difficulties. Notice the student's miscues or errors as you progress. Under ideal conditions, teach one new mini lesson at a time; stay with only a few concepts per day, one per teaching session. Each mini lesson lasts only fifteen to twenty minutes to maintain interest.

The Learning Sequence

Consonants

These are letters that are not vowels.

- Fourteen of these always have their own unique sounds:
  b, d, f, h, j, k, l, m, n, p, r, t, v, and *z*

- Emphasize the next six:

  c, g, q, s, y, and *w* have different sounds.
- There are eight digraphs:

  ch, sh, th, wh, ph, gh, ck, and *ng*
- And there are two-letter blends and three-letter blends: Blends can appear almost anywhere in a word. When they occur at the beginning of words or syllables, they are called *initial blends* (like the *cr* in *cr*eam). When they are at the end, they are called *final blends* (like the *st* in la*st*). Blends are also found in the middle of words and are called *medial* (like the *scr* in de*scr*ibe).

Vowels

- Short (soft) vowels: *a, e, i, o, u* (and sometimes *y* and *w* when other letters are added)
- Long (hard) vowels: A, E, I, O, and U
- Vowel teams: *ae, ai, ee, ea, ie, oa, ei, ue, ui, ey, ew, au,* and *aw.*

Special Sounds

- The Special E: Placed at the end of a word, it becomes silent but creates a different word with the first vowel being pronounced as hard: *at+e* = *ate* or *mat+e* = *mate*. ("E on the end makes the first vowel long.")
- The Bossy R (also called the R-Controlled Vowel): *ar, er, ir, or,* or *ur.* It is also called vowel plus *r.*
- Diphthongs: *oi, ou, ow, oo,* and *oy.*
- And, finally, there are irregular sounds, exceptions to the rules that can be learned as they are encountered.

Structural Analysis

- **Word Families** (See CSML-022)

  About fifty word families make up more than five hundred English words. Using the patterns listed in CSML-022 allows you to form countless words. Sometimes word families are called phonograms or rhyming words. In

41

building these words, the beginning is called the *onset*, and the rhyming pattern is called the *rime*.

- **Compound Words** (See CSML-023)
  Compound words are two words that are put together to form a new word. These are side-by-side words. To remember what they are, simply say, "You take two words and squash them together." CSML-23 shows how to start with concrete objects or drawing compound word parts, and look for basic compound words.

- **Affixes (root words) with prefixes and suffixes** (See CSML-024)
  Affixes are like train cars. When these are in front of the engine, they're called the root word, or prefixes. When they follow it, they are known as suffixes. The word *affix* means to connect or add on, to take a syllable and add it on to the front of a root word. The word syllable *pre* comes from Latin and means "to go before." When you add the syllable *pre* to the word *fix*, it becomes prefix, something added before a word, to create a new word with a new meaning. A suffix is exactly the opposite. It is a *fix* following the root word, to creating a new word with a new meaning.

- **Contractions** (See CSML-025)
  A contraction is a short form of two words. The words are put together like a compound word and then one or more letters are removed and replaced by an apostrophe. For example, *we are* becomes *weare*, and then the *a* is removed and replaced by the apostrophe ('), which leaves the contraction *we're*. *She is* becomes *sheis*, and then the *i* is removed and replaced by an apostrophe ('), which leaves the contraction *she's*.

- **Syllables** (See CSML-026)

  CSML-026 describes how to teach syllables. A syllable is a part of a word. As a matter of fact, in some cases, a syllable *is* the word (like *A* or *I*). But usually a syllable (word part) is made up of a vowel sound and one or more consonants. Then each word is made up of one or more syllables.

CSML-008: SOUNDING OUT NEW WORDS

Systematic Phonics Sequence 2

Introduction

Word recognition is the beginning of the reading process. Reading Champions are word detectives who are learning letters and combinations of letters. The systematic phonics sequence works most of the time to sound out new, unknown words. Easy to master rules are listed and explained throughout the Easy-Start mini lessons.

A basic understanding of these rules makes it easy to figure out many new words. Some English words are irregular; the language is not completely phonetic. Nonetheless, knowledge of phonics is essential because there is enough consistency; time-tested phonics rules apply at least 65 percent of the time. When exceptions occur, say to your student, "This is an exception," and use another method.

Why Do We Need to Know This?

Having a systematic approach is extremely important. Easy-Start sequence for teaching and learning letters and their associated sounds, including:

1. Consonants that usually sound the same (CSML-010)
2. The remaining single consonants (CSML-011)
3. The short vowels (CSML-014)
4. The long vowels (CSML-015)
5. The remaining special sounds (CSML-020)

Each sound is accompanied by one or two key words.

Students learn to break down long words into their component parts (known as syllables) to unlock or decode unfamiliar words. This skill is called "structural analysis," which includes compound words, syllables, contractions, word families, root words, prefixes, and suffixes.

In order to start blending sounds into words early in the instruction sequence, add vowels after several consonants are known. As quickly as possible, make and read new words by substituting the initial letters to form other words.

Examples: Using the seed pair *ig*, words like *big, dig, fig, jig, pig, rig, wig*, and *zig* will provide a means of demonstrating how easily words can be built. Then simply by substituting the vowel *a* in place of *I*, you can get *bag, jag, rag, wag*, and *zag*; then add *gag, hag, lag, nag, sag*, and *tag*. (Are *zig* and *zag* legitimate words? Check them out in a dictionary).

Assignment: Write down as many words as you can for the seed words *...ag* and *...op*.

For another exercise, students start doing partial reading of texts containing one-syllable words (and there are many of these). As an example, there are seventeen one-syllable words in the preceding sentence.

Note to Coaches

Expect rapid progress when students learn some of the same-sound consonants right away, but these generally cannot be used to construct real words. Avoid nonsense words. Use correct models. Include both short and long vowels as soon as possible.

If practicing words for which the student has just learned the rules, provide cues to help with sounding out the word rather than correcting each mispronounced word (see The Cueing Process: CSML-006). Deal separately with non- phonic, irregular words that do not follow the rules as sight words. Pronounce them the first time or two, and say, "These are exceptions."

When reviewing, include a spelling activity. As your student learns to unlock new words by sounding, model how to simultaneously apply these new skills when spelling. It is a great help in being able to handle a new word and determine its pronunciation or meaning using this analysis.

Tried and true phonics clues will help in pronouncing little words, and they will help in pronouncing longer words. Frequently, a clue helps with a syllable, and the syllable can help unlock an entire word.

CSML-009: TEACHING NEW SOUNDS AND LETTERS

Systematic Phonics Sequence 3

Introduction

This brief section provides a ten-part teaching lesson format and practice exercises for learning new sounds and letters. Review sounds from previously learned lessons, letters, words, concepts, or patterns.

In the CSML lesson plan format, this appears as "Prerequisites for Learning."

1. Provide a strong set or opener to create interest and motivate the student. In the CSML format, this usually appears under the "Why do I need to know this?" heading.
2. Introduce the new sound, letter, word, concept, or pattern to be taught in the current lesson.
3. Share reading of the new material (story, article, or textbook portion) that reinforces the instructional set.
4. Find other examples of the concept in print, in books, or by "reading the room" wall-print (refer to print-rich environment).
5. Do a strong review of, or close to, the instructional set. In some cases, this might consist of pointing out why this new knowledge

will be useful to the student. (Refer to the "Why do I have to learn this?" section.)

6. Continue reinforcement with practice, drill, and repetition.

7. Continually check for understanding; aim for mastery.

8. Re-teach, if needed, and close with a brief review of everything taught. Then proceed to the new sound, letter, word, concept, or pattern in the next lesson.

9. Record what was covered in the lesson, strategies you used, and the results of the instruction.

10. Decide what you will teach next based on the prior lesson.

Prerequisites for Learning

Throughout the Reading Champs Easy-Start Mini Lesson Series, each lesson or activity is based on the student's prior knowledge. Sequential learning activities build on former known information.

All instruction, whether verbal or written, uses English as a primary language. The student must have adequate basic language skills. Before starting any language instruction, it is important to ensure that the student has the visual and hearing ability to see and hear well. In addition, at each new step in the process, you may want to conduct brief IRIs (Informal Reading Inventories) to determine the student's rate of progress.

Why Do We Need to Know This?

We need to know and practice it to be better at speaking, reading, and writing.

Sounding out words or the application of phonetic principles to help recognize new words is useful for between at least 65 percent and possibly 85 percent of words. Having a systematic approach is extremely important when sounding out unfamiliar words.

One of these approaches is the Easy-Start sequence for teaching and learning letters and their associated sounds. These success secrets make a big difference in your teaching. Most letters, and their associated sounds, are fairly easy to understand, but there are exceptions to almost every rule. These exceptions will be explained as they occur, but some are important enough to be taught separately, or use other methods.

Learning Activities

When teaching a new letter or sound, be sure the student can hear the sound and tell it apart from other sounds. For example, as you begin to teach the letter *b*, say, "Listen to the sound of these *b* words: *Bill, boy, baseball, bat,* and *bounce.* Tell me the words that start with the *b* sound."

Next, say words with the same sound and include one or two that don't. Make sure the student knows the difference. Say, "Pickles, pears, peas, apples, and bugs. Which words sound like the *p* we practiced? Which words don't share the *p* sound?" (*Bugs* is the only correct answer because a*pp*le does have the *p* sound, just not at the beginning.)

Involve the senses as you associate a letter with a sound. As age appropriate, write the letter in the air, on a white board or piece of paper, in sand or clay, using Play-Doh, pipe cleaners, or wax sticks.

Here's another helpful hint for dealing with a noisy environment or short attention spans. Students will be surprised (and usually excited) to hear the magnified sound when using a "phonics phone," or plumber's elbow with a flexible tube. (Check out hardware stores). Placed next to the ear, this simple and inexpensive tool really amplifies the sound.

A good, easy, attention-getting activity is to model—and then have the students do the same thing—placing a clean piece of tissue directly in front of the mouth. It is interesting to see and feel the air flow while saying voiced and unvoiced sounds. To help in understanding the concept, place the palm of your hand in front of your mouth and say, "*Think* and *this*."

Another activity that works well when teaching a tactile-kinesthetic (TK) learner is to use a prop to make learning fun and help make the association with sound, letter, and the representative object. You might *b*ounce a *b*all while emphasizing the *b* sound, or you could connect each sound and letter with a corresponding body part. For example, point to your ear and say, "*E* as in *e*ar." (Note: select words that present the dominant (hard) sound: *s* as in *s*ew, *n* as in *n*ose, etc.)

Here's a little ditty created especially for a friend's infant son (many years ago).

These are my eyes, and this is my nose
These are my fingers, and these are my toes
These are my ears, and this is my chin
And this is my mouth, where the food goes in …
To the belly, belly, belly, belly, belly!

There was much tickling and giggling. It was a great way for his mother to introduce him to Dr. Seuss.

Always associate a sound with its letter and a key word. It is helpful to enhance learning with a picture or photo of the word to illustrate the letter and the sound. Another effective practice is to go hands-on by using magnetic or other letters and, especially, three-dimensional blocks or cubes. And there is always the cut-out paper letter if space is limited or you don't have a steel wall or file cabinet where you can hang magnets.

Additional Learning Activities

Working with a student, write a list of words that begin with one letter. For example, using a *d*, pronounce each word as you write it, then, ask your student to pronounce it. Say, "Point out in what way the words sound and look the same." "Do they all start with the same sound?" "Which words sound alike?" "What is the middle sound?" "What are the beginning and ending sounds?" "Do you know any other word yet that shares this same sound?"

Summary

Sounding out words or the application of general principles to help recognize new words is useful for at least 65 percent of words. Instructors should be sure to model and practice the letter and sound together with its key word and an illustration.

When students are ready to sound out words using the new sound, present the new letter (and sound) in one-syllable words and associate it with sounds they have already learned. Next, blend it together into a recognized word, such as / m / a / t / = mat.

As soon as the new sound is recognized in words, begin practicing the sound in sentences. Initially, prepare sentences that use the same sounds frequently. Here are some examples that use the hard *c* (/ k /). "Cathy caught the cat in her car." "Bill is at bat, but Bob bats a bit better."

Because some students take longer than others to learn new sounds and letters, use lots of drill and practice using multisensory methods. The repetition does help. Remain patient, and enjoy watching your Reading Champ in training.

Finally, the three types of word recognition techniques are overlapping, but all are necessary for teaching decoding skills. These include providing many visual clues, emphasis on meaning, and analytical procedures such as sight words, context cues, and word parts.

CSML-010: CONSONANTS THAT SOUND THE SAME

Systematic Phonics Sequence 4

Introduction

The English alphabet is made up of twenty-six letters. Of these, five (*a, e, i, o,* and *u*) are regular vowels and two (*y* and *w*) are semi-vowels. Semi-vowels are letters used as vowels in certain situations. The remaining letters in the alphabet are consonants.

Our language would be much simpler to master if each letter had only one sound. However, some of the letters have more than one sound. Learning the sounds of letters takes place in stages, each building upon those previously learned. Easy-Start mini lessons make the learning sensible.

Knowing the sounds of individual letters can make recognizing unknown words much easier. The first category to be learned is the fifteen consonant sounds that are consistent and usually remain the same. These consonant letters are: *b, d, f, h, j, k, l, m, n, p, r, t, v, z,* and (usually) *w*.

Once students learn these fifteen sounds, they have mastered more than one-third of the sounds in the English language! They also learn an important tool for constructing simple single syllable words.

Prerequisites for Learning

As we indicated in section 9, all Reading Champs instruction, whether verbal or written, is provided in English as the primary language. Before starting any language instruction, it is important to ensure that the student has the visual and hearing ability to see and hear well.

Why Do We Need to Know This?

As we said in the introduction, the first category of sounds and their corresponding letters to be learned are the fifteen consonants whose sounds are consistent and remain the same in most cases. These consonant letters are: *b, d, f, h, j, k, l, m, n, p, r, t, v, z,* and (usually) *w*.

Once students learn these fifteen consonants, they have mastered more than half of the letters and one-third of the sounds used in the English language. They also have an important tool for constructing simple (single-syllable) words. Students from the earliest learning understand that letters—whether consonants or vowels—do not stand alone. They must be combined with other letters and sounds to make words and sentences.

Learning Activities

When teaching letters, be sure the student can hear the sound and tell it apart from other sounds. Now, as we focus on the first fifteen consonants, we use association of a sound with its letter and a key word. We should also begin identifying the sound and the letter in the beginning, middle, or end of words.

It is helpful to enhance learning with a familiar picture or photo of the word to illustrate the letter and the sound. Throughout this learning activity, continue to use the reinforcement techniques presented in section 9. For example, write a list of words beginning with one letter.

For example, use a *d* as in *David*. Pronounce each word as you write it, and then ask your student to pronounce it. But be careful when choosing words; in some uses, the letter may be silent (like the second *d* is in dodgeball / *dojbal* /). If this happens, simply explain silent letters and give a few other examples.

Again, say, "Point out in what way the words sound and look the same," and then ask questions as you go along. "Do they all start with the same sound?" "Which words sound alike?" "What is the middle sound? (*In dodgeball, it is silent.*)" "What are the beginning and ending sounds?" "Do you know any other word yet that shares this same sound?"

Group known sight words with a common consonant (with a common beginning sound), such as *bat*, *bit*, and *but*. Point out how the *b* sound remains the same—even in *baseball*, *bunny*, and *beanbag*.

Point out that the initial letters of the word are the same, and the sounds are alike. Tell the name of the letter while writing or tracing it on a piece of paper in both uppercase and lowercase letters (so the students can see the visual difference but understand the sound does not change). Here is one list, but feel free to make your own. And by all means, encourage students to make up their own lists, including their own names. It is best to teach uppercase and lowercase letters at the same time!

- B / b   Ben, Bob, Barbara, Betsey, Barney, baby, ball, baboon, balloon, Band-Aid.
- D / d   David, Donald, Diane, dog, deer, desk, dinner, donkey, door, drink, duck.
- F / f   Frank, Fiona, face, far, fat, fire, fireman, fish, five, flag, four.
- H / h   Henry, Howard, Honey (a girl's name), hair, hat, head, hill, hole, home, horse.
- J / j   James, Julie, jump, jigsaw.
- K / k   Kenneth, Kathleen, kangaroo, ketchup, key, kite, knife (silent 'k').
- L / l   Luke, Leon, Lois, ladder, lamp, lawn, leg, lemon, light, lion, lock.
- M / m   Matthew, Michael, Molina, man, market, mat, meat.
- N / n   Nancy, Nathan, Noel, neck, nose, night, nine, new, net.
- P / p   Paul, Phillip, Pauline, pants, paper, pen, pet, pig, pizza, policeman, pony.
- R / r   Ralph, Rose, Raphael, rabbit, red, ring, river, road, rock, roof.

- T / t   Timothy, Theresa, ten, three, tiger, train, tree, truck, two.
- V / v   Vanessa, Victor, van, vice, video.
- W / w William, Wanda, Walter, walk, wash, water, wave, wind, wolf, worm.
- Z / z   Zebra, zoo.

Additional Learning Activities

It is not too early to begin teaching students how to use a dictionary to sound out words and find out which two-letter combinations almost never start a word. Ask the student to give you two letters (from the list of fifteen you are using) (for example *k* and *x*), then look in the dictionary to try to find words beginning with either *kx* or *xk*. (There aren't any.) Or in the case of *t* and *h* (*th*—there are many or *ht*—again, none there). However, your primary focus should be on correct models that are consistent, and please do not use any nonsense words. You can now understand why.

And *th* gives you an excellent introduction into the consonant digraph section, which is still a few lessons in the future.

Summary

Remember what we said in section 9? Sounding out words or the application of general principles to help recognize new words is useful most of the time. Instructors should be sure to model and practice the letter and sound together with its key word and an illustration.

When students are ready to sound out words using the new sound, present the new letter (and sound) in one-syllable words and associate it with sounds they have already learned. Next, blend it together into a recognized word, such as / m / a / t / = mat.

As soon as the new sound is recognized in words, begin practicing the sound in sentences. Initially, prepare sentences that use the same sounds frequently. For example, use the hard *c* (/ k /) "Cathy caught the cat in her car" and "Bill is at bat, but Bob bats a bit better."

Because some students take longer than others to learn new sounds and letters, use lots of drill and practice with multisensory methods. The repetition does help. Remain patient, and enjoy watching your Reading Champ in training.

Finally, the three types of word recognition techniques are overlapping, but all are necessary for teaching decoding skills. These include providing many visual clues, emphasis on meaning, and analytical procedures, such as sight words, context cues, and word parts.

Note to Coaches

Practice each type of strategy in various written materials. Start with easy text and progress to more difficult (and challenging) reading materials. Cueing can provide extremely valuable skills if they are reviewed and practiced at each progressive learning level and across every level of content.

CSML-011: REMAINING SINGLE CONSONANTS

Systematic Phonics Sequence 5

Introduction

The remaining consonants have more than one sound and are called *consonant equivalents*. Model these consonant sounds, including key words. For example, pair the *hard C* with the word *cat* (the *k* sound) and the *soft C* would be modeled with *cent* (the *s* sound). A *hard G* is heard in the word *golf* (a guttural *g*) while the *soft G* sounds the name *George* (*j*).

S is inconsistent. Sometimes *s* has its own sound (like the *s* in *sunshine*) but it can also have a *zee* sound (as in *always*). When sounding out a word, always try the *soft s* first. If it does not sound right, then use the hard *z*. Any plurals formed by adding *s* to the singular root almost always use a *hard s*.

Next, practice the letter *Y*, which has three sounds. It can have the sound of a *long i* (as in the word *cry*); it could have the sound of a *long e* (as in the word *city*); or says its own name (in the word *yellow*).

Prerequisites for Learning

As we indicated in sections 9 and 10, all Reading Champs instruction, whether verbal or written, is in English. Before starting *any* language instruction, it is important to ensure that the student has good vision and hearing. There are few prerequisites as we are still learning the fundamental building blocks of formal language and reading instruction.

Why Do We Need to Know This?

Not all letters have only one sound. Some have two, and some have three or more sounds; sometimes a letter may have no sound at all. For example, *h* is often silent, as in the word *ghost*. Knowing some Easy-Start rules increases reading fluency and comprehension.

Instructional Activity

Learning Activities

Make a chart on a piece of paper, with three columns. List the three sounds, one at the top of each column (*Y* as in yellow; *Y* as in city; *Y* as in cry).

- Using a student's personal vocabulary or reading instructional materials, create lists of *y* words and place under the proper heading. When a word, such as *yearly* has two different sounds for the letter in the same word, list that word twice.

Y (yellow)	Y (city)	Y (cry)
yesterday yearly	baby yearly	fly

Figure 11-1: Single Consonant Chart Template

- The consonant *Q/q* is always followed by the vowel *u*, as in queen or quiet. ("Q and *u* get married"). While reading, find as many

Qu/qu words as possible, and either make a list in a notebook or create a series of flash cards or word rings.

- When *W/w* has another letter placed in front of it, it becomes a vowel diphthong; as an example, think of *ow* as in "Ow! That hurt me." Or in the word *owl*. There is also another *ow* sound, the long *o* sound as in *blow* or *flow*. Also, it can be silent as in the *w* in *wring* or *wrist*.

- *X/x* has no sound of its own (other than the name of the letter and when it is hyphenated as in the case of *X-ray*. But it combines with other letters in special cases to form the *ks* sound as in extra or extreme, or the *gz* sound as in exact, or the *z* sound found in *xylophone* and *Xerox* (pronounced *zee-rocks*). Find the letter *x* in other reading.

In each of the four rule exercises, it helps to create charts illustrating the concept being taught. These charts (tables) are also great study aids for future reviews.

Additional Learning Activities

Find words matching the various special consonant sounds listed above. Review these phonics clues:

- The letter *G* can have either a hard (*g* as in *golf*) or soft (*j* as in *gem* (sounds like *jem*).
- The letter *G* followed by *E, I,* or *Y* usually has a *J* sound. Otherwise, it has the hard *G* sound.
- The letter *C* can have either a hard (*c / k /* as in *Columbia*) or soft *c* as in *city* (sounds like *sitee*).
- The letter *C* followed by *E, I,* or *Y* usually has an *S* sound. Otherwise, it has the *K* sound.
- The letter *Q* has no sound of its own. When followed by a *U,* it has the *kw* sound (as the words *quack* and *quarter*).
- Consonants are sometimes silent, not sounded. As examples: the *b* in lam*b*, the *h* in *h*our, and the *k* in *k*now.

Summary

As we said in sections 9 and 10, applying general principles for sounding out words helps recognize at least 65 percent—and as high as 85 percent—of words, which is enough "utility" to make a difference. Instructors/coaches should be sure to model for the student. Provide sufficient practice of the letter and its correct sound together with its key word and an illustration.

As soon as new sounds are recognized and identified in words, begin practicing the sound in sentences.

Remember to do lots of drill and practice using multisensory methods. Repetition does help memorization. Then, as a Reading Champs coach, your main job is to remain patient and enjoy helping your Reading Champ in training.

CSML-012: CONSONANT BLENDS

Systemic Phonics Sequence 6

Introduction

Consonant blends are two or three side-by-side consonants that blend into one new sound. You still hear each of the sounds. Think of blending sounds into a blender. The examples below are common combinations:

sl as in *slide*	*fl* as in *fleece*	*sp* as in *spoon*
pr as in *prize*	*gl* as in *glide*	*st* as in *street*
cr as in *cradle*	*sk* as in *skinny*	*spl* as in *splash*
fr as in *frosty*	*sm* as in *smart*	*spr* as in *spring*
br as in *breeze*	*sn* as in *snap*	*str* as in *strong*
tw as in *twin*	*sw* as in *sweet*	*nk* as in *ink*
pl as in *please*	*gr* as in *grapefruit*	*ng* as in *sing*
cl as in *class*	*dr* as in *dress*	*nt* as in *plant*
bl as in *blue*	*tr* as in *tree*	*nd* as in *bend*

Figure 12-1: Consonant Blends

Instructional Activity

Consonant blends are the phonic equivalent of fresh chocolate milk. You take two good ingredients (fresh milk and chocolate syrup) and mix them together to make something more flavorful than either one separately. What would the English language be like without these versatile sound combinations? Check out the following teaching tips:

Blends almost always sound the same wherever they appear. Here are a few guidelines to use when identifying and decoding blends:

- The *l*, *r*, and *s* blends are most often found at the beginning or middle of a word, but can also be at the end.
- *T* blends are found in the beginning and the ending of many words.
- *D* and *p* blends are usually found at the ends of words.

Prerequisites for Learning

At this point, students need to recognize most of the consonants. Blends help rapid decoding of sight words, which supports comprehension and fluency (reading rate).

Why Do We Need to Know This?

You also need to know this. If you were to try to blend, for example, *c* and *p* into a single blended sound, it simply would not make sense. Knowing what does and doesn't work makes language acquisition simpler. Understanding that *pl* as in *please* and *apple* and *pr* as in *prize* works, but *pt* is a real tongue twister, which is why the *p* in this combination is almost always silent.

Learning Activities

Blends appear almost anywhere in a word. When they are at the beginning of words or syllables, they are called *initial blends* (like the *cr* in *cream*). When they are at the end, they are called *final blends* (like the *st* in *last*).

Blends found in the middle of words are called *medial* (like the *scr* in de*scr*ibe).

Helpful Hint for Learners

When dividing words into syllables, blends are not separated. Make flash cards to practice these common blends.

Example, SL = Slide, sleep, slip, sled, sloppy, sling.

- *PR* = Print, press, pretty, proud, praise.
- *CR* = Creep, crush, crop, crisp, crust, cramp, crash, crazy.
- *FR* = Fresh, friend, from, free, fright, frog, fry, freeze.
- *BR* = Bread, broke, brand, brake, break, bring, brush, branch, brick, brown.
- *GR* = Grand, groan, grass, green, grape, grill, grin, grab, ground.
- *TR* = True, tree, track, trick, train, truck, trap, treat, trip, try.
- *DR* = Drive, dress, dream, drill, drink, draw, drive, drag.
- *SP* = Spell, spill, speak, speech, spin, spark, spend, spot.
- *ST* = Stand, still, stain, stone, stack, stage, start, star, steam, stamp.
- *ST* = Fast, first, last, lost, most, least.
- *SM* = Small, smell, smile, smash, smooth, smudge.
- *SP* = Split, splash, splinter, spray.

Additional Learning Activities

Using a variety of written materials, look for words with one of the above listed blend sounds. Decide whether these are initial (at the beginning), medial (in the middle), or final (at the end) blends.

And, finally, find and list blend words for each of the major blend combinations.

Summary

As the above list demonstrates, consonant blends are parts of many words in the English language.

CSML-013: CONSONANT DIGRAPHS

Systemic Phonics Sequence 7

Introduction

In the last Mini lesson, you practiced consonant blends, two or three consonant sounds blended together. There are also double consonants with a single sound. These are called *digraphs*. Digraphs are two letters with one sound. Examples are *th, wh, sh, ph,* and *ch*. You hear one new sound, not the two individual letters. Reminder, with blends, you hear the two or three distinct sounds, which is quite different than digraphs.

A digraph is usually found at the beginning or the end of a word (in the case of the word *church*, at both ends of the word).

The most common digraphs are: *sh* as in *show*, *ch* as in *church*, *th* as in *think, this,* and *that*, and *wh* as in *what* and *where*. However, there are other digraphs, not as common, but just as important to know.

Although each of these is a pair of letters, the pair stands for one sound. *Ph* (an *f* sound as in *phone*), *ng* (as in *song*—or twice in *singing*), and gh (an *f* sound as in *tough* or silent as in *through*).

Prerequisites for Learning

We are ready to recognize most of the consonants, some of the rules for working with them, and a few exceptions that make the English language more fun—more challenging, but more fun! Remember that digraphs are part of the key to rapid decoding of sight words, which supports comprehension and reading fluency (rate).

Why Do We Need to Know This?

Consonant digraphs are far more than two random consonants standing next to each other. From a linguistic point of view, they provide a phonic structure that is compatible to the components of sounds. If you were to try to blend *c* and *p* into a single blended sound, it simply would not work. Knowing what works and what doesn't will make the process of language acquisition much simpler.

Instructional Activity

If consonant blends are the phonic equivalent of fresh chocolate milk, consonant digraphs are the *wh*ipped cream and *ch*erry. You take two good ingredients (fresh milk and chocolate syrup) and mix them together to make something that is more flavorful than either one separately.

For the most part, they usually always make the same sound no matter where they appear. There are glaring differences, like *ch* (in chart, chew, nachos, cheese, and chair) and *ch* (in *Chevrolet* which sounds like *Shevrolet*) but that's an English thing because in Spanish, it is properly pronounced *Chevrolet*!

Here are a few guidelines to remember.

- *Sh* is almost always the same as the keywords *ship*, *sheep*, *shoulder*, *fish*, and *wash*. (Remember what we learned in session 5? *S* blends are most often found at the beginning or middle of a word but can also be found at the end).

- *Ch* digraphs actually have three sounds. The most common is that found in *ch*icken, *ch*ew, and bea*ch*. It can also be represented in words like *Ch*ristmas (the *k* sound). The least common is the *sh* sound heard in *ch*ef and *ch*ute.

Learning Activities

Like consonant blends, consonant digraphs appear almost anywhere in a word. When they are at the beginning of words or syllables, they are called *initial digraphs* (like the *ch* in *ch*icken or *ch*urch). When they are at the end, they are called *final digraphs* (like the *ch* in pat*ch* or wat*ch*). Medial (middle of word) digraphs are seldom seen but do exist.

Helpful Hint for Learners

Just like when dividing words with blends into syllables, *consonant digraphs are not separated* (because they present an undivided sound). Make flash cards to practice these common digraphs and develop them into another strong set to build your sight-word library.

- *Sh* = *(almost always the same sound)* shop, shoe, ship, sheep, shore, shout, shell, shape, cash, fish, short.
- *Ch* = *(almost always the same sound)* nachos, church, cheese, chimp, chimney, chill, chip, chow, chin.
- *Th* = *(almost always the same sound)* think, thin, thick, fifth, forth, fourth, thank, this, that, teeth, these, sixth.
- *Wh* = *(almost always the same sound but may have a silent w)* which, what, who, when, where, why, whose, wheat, whisper, wheel.
- *Ph* = *(almost always the same f sound)* phone, pharmacy, gopher, alphabet.
- *Gh* = *(two sounds but inconsistent)* though, through, thorough, cough, tough, rough, enough, laugh.
- *Ng* = *(almost always the same sound)* ring, rang, sling, fling, spring, king, string, thing, wing, sang.

Additional Learning Activities

Then, using a variety of written materials, look for and list words that have one of the above consonant digraph sounds. Decide whether these are initial, medial, or final digraphs.

Next, make two columns on a piece of paper. Head one "Voiced TH" and the other "Unvoiced TH." Unvoiced means the vocal cords do not vibrate. Write down which of the following words do you think would be listed under each column: thick, thin, though worth, brother, third, smooth, with, thank, other. Explain the reasons for your choices. Then find additional *th* words and add to the lists.

Finally, *wh*en you are *through wit*h *th*at exercise, write a sentence *sh*owi*ng* your understandi*ng* of digra*ph*s, *wh*ich contains at least one word for ea*ch* of *th*e seven digra*ph* categories.

For more practice, write a paragraph.

Summary

The exercise demonstrates how often we use digraphs in our everyday lives without giving them a passing thought. It also concludes the phonics elements dealing with consonants and how they (and their sounds) are used to create spoken and written communications in the English language.

CSML-014: SHORT VOWELS

Systematic Phonics Sequence 8

Introduction

When consistent consonants with one sound are known, teach short vowels. By adding a vowel with the consonant/s, your student makes and reads new words! The most common vowel sound is the short vowel, referred to as "unglided" because it stands alone as a single sound. In the dictionary, vowels are tagged with diacritical marks; the short vowel tag looks like a half circle over the vowel.

Since every word in the English language contains at least one vowel, knowing the five major vowel sounds is critical. Most short vowel sounds are consistent:

- A (a) as in apple
- E (e) as in egg
- I (i) as in igloo
- O (o) as in ox (sound is similar to *ah*)
- U (u) as in umbrella

In a dictionary, if you notice an *a* with a dot over it, this is an *Italian a*, as the word sof*a*. Other examples of the Italian *a* are tub*a*, *a*lert, *a*dore, *a*rithmetic, and pand*a*.

Learning about vowels begins with several basic statements.

- Every word and syllable in the English language contains at least one vowel.
- There are five vowels and two semi-vowels (which will be covered later) in the English language.
- Every vowel has at least two sounds, short and long.
- Vowels are one of the language elements that come to us, almost unchanged, from the Greeks. Vowels make it possible for a language with only twenty-six letters to make over ten thousand common words!
- Without vowels, the English language could not be learned (and spoken) as easily as it is.

Prerequisites for Learning

The student knows all twenty-six letters and primary sounds of the English alphabet at sight. This can be verified very quickly with an alphabet flash card set.

Why Do We Need to Know This?

This knowledge is necessary for communicating in the English language, in either a spoken or written form.

Reminder: Every word and syllable in the English language contains at least one vowel. Every vowel has at least two sounds, short and long.

Instructional Activity

Clues within a syllable or word (context) tell whether a vowel is short or long. The most reliable is where it appears in each syllable.

One way to guess whether a vowel is short is to break the word into parts, its syllables. Since every syllable has a vowel in it, when the vowel is in the middle of a syllable, it is usually short.

Helpful Hint for Learners

Learn this short vowel rule: "A vowel usually has a short sound if it is in the beginning or middle, not at the end of a word, especially when the word has only one syllable."

Some examples of this rule in action are: *and, at, cat, an, man, end, bend, leg, beg, fan, lip, hop, up,* and *under.*

Primary Sounds of the Short Vowels

Start by learning the short *a* sound. Every time you are learning a sound, use a key word, a picture, a photo, or some other concrete object to reinforce the pronunciation. For example, the words *lap* or *back.* As you say the sound, point to a person's or your lap or back.

Next, model how this new sound, placed between the sounds of two known consonants, makes a word. Use letter tiles (like those in a Scrabble game), alphabet cards, cubes, magnetic letters create a word, such as *at,* and then add a letter in front to make the word *cat.*

Now continue substituting the first letter and creating new words: fat, hat, mat, pat, rat, sat, and vat. That gives you eight words, all properly spelled and pronounced. Now *that* is reading!

Let's try it with the other vowels.

- *E* as in *leg*
- *I* as in *lip* or *hit*

Notice how changing the vowel gives you two new words. Change the *i* to an *a*, and you go from *lip* to *lap* or *hit* to *hat.*

The key word for the short *o* might be *knock* (Tap *on* the table top).

The word for *u* might be *up* and you point *up* as you say the word.

As you progress, build onto your word list (or sight-word flash cards). They make great practice tools.

Additional Learning Activities

Print the letters studied and find them in a variety of other printed materials. Then match simple words with their short vowel sounds.

- *a*: man, pan, pat, sat, rat, lap, back, nap, rap, tap, snap, sad, pad, cat.
- *e*: men, pet, leg, fed, wed, led, shed, red, hen, then, ten, pen, wet, set.
- *i*: lip, tip, rip, nip, lit, sit, pin, ring, sing, sting, wing, king, lid, trip, fin.
- *o*: knock, rock, sock, pop, stop, top, not, dot, hop, shop, chop, drop, mop.
- *u*: up, sun, fun, bun, mud, pup, tub, cut, us, bus, hum, chum, nut, cub.

Starting with short *a* words, ask the students, "How are these words alike?" "What is the sound you hear?" "Let's read all these words together."

Underline each vowel that has a short vowel sound and tell what the vowel is: *cat, cup, fun, rot, stop, sit, drop, lip, hat, pat, pan, pin, pen, ran, pop, rub.*

Make the letters in each group into a word using a short vowel sound.

- *m-d, p-t, b-d, r-n, s-p, w-nt, b-mp, c-p, s-t, h-t, p-t, r-p, r-t, m-t, t-p*

Practice reading and writing these Easy-Start words. Are all the vowel sounds long or short?

- A: mad, bad, at, sad, am, cat, rat, pat, lap, back, map, rap, tap, snap, sad
- E: men, pet, leg, fed, wed, shed, red, hen, then, ten, pen, net, wet, set.
- I: lip, tip, rip, nip, lit, sit, pin, ring, sing, sting, wing, king, lid, trip, fin.
- O: knock, rock, sock, pop, stop, top, not, dot, hop, shop, chop, drop, mop.
- U: up, sun, fun, mud, pup, tub, cut, us, bus, hum, chum, nut, cub, bud.

In the following words, underline each vowel that has a short sound.

- cap, cape, cup, clean, drop, team, tent, ham, came, toast, cub

Summary

There are clues within a syllable or word that tell whether a vowel is short or long. The most reliable is where it appears in the individual syllable.

One way to guess whether a vowel is short is to break the word into parts. Since every syllable has a vowel in it, when the vowel is in the middle of a syllable, it is usually short.

Helpful Hint for Learners

Learn this short vowel rule. "A vowel usually has a short sound if it is in the beginning or middle and not at the end of a word, especially when the word has only one syllable."

CSML-015: LONG VOWELS

Systemic Phonics Sequence 9

Introduction

When a vowel is at the end of a syllable, it usually has a long sound. This is an *open* syllable. Short vowels are referred to as *closed* syllables. Examples are *I, me, she, no, go,* and *so.* Long vowels say their own names:

- A (a) as in acorn
- E (e) as in eat
- I (i) as in Idaho
- O (o) as in oak
- U (u) as in unicorn

Because the names of the long vowels are the same as their sounds, they are easy to learn. Long vowels are really interesting. There are more variations than with short vowel sounds. Some words have two vowels in the middle or end with the letter *e*. These are called *vowel teams* [ie, e, ee (meet), ea (team), and the *Special E* (kite)] and are learned a little later in the instructional sequence.

Other interesting vowel combinations include *vowel digraphs*. You may remember digraphs from Phonics Element 6: "A digraph is two letters, standing next to each other, with one sound that is generally quite different from either of the two letters." Some special vowel digraphs are *au, aw, eu, ew,* and *ey.* In addition, there are two other special cases: The R-Controlled Vowels (*ar, er, ir, or,* and *ur*). And vowel diphthongs (*oy* as in boy and *oi* as in boil).

Prerequisites for Learning

Students should know the names of all twenty-six letters and the primary sounds of the English alphabet on sight. This can be verified very quickly with an alphabet flash card set.

Why Do We Need to Know This?

Because the English language is so versatile, almost every letter uses several different sounds, depending on other letters and sounds around it. This is especially true when working with long vowels. Just because the names of the long vowels are easy to master (their primary sounds are the same as the letter name) does not mean that they will always sound the same. As an example of this, take a look at the word *boat.* In this case, the second vowel is silent. If not, it would have to be pronounced as "boe-ate."

But, happily, there are only a few rules that need to be learned to make vowels manageable.

Learning Activities

When learning other letters and sounds, each long vowel sound should be matched with at least one key word. The rules for word selection are also the same as in earlier lessons: concrete objects, body parts, and other familiar concepts you can point at when you say the word.

- A as in *a*pe or t*a*ble (point to or touch the table).
- E as in h*ea*r or *ea*ting (make a motion like putting food into your mouth).

- I as in *ice* cube or *I* (I point to myself).
- O as in *open* or *pose* (I put my hands together and then open them).
- U as in *unicorn* (I make my finger look like a single horn on my forehead).

Note: Reading Champs' Word Wall Alphabet cards (example on page 24) are very effective in this exercise as well.

Helpful Hint for Learners

When a vowel is at the end of a syllable, and is the only vowel in the syllable, the vowel is usually long. In a dictionary, the diacritical mark looks like a line or dash above the vowel.

- In the word *go*, the *o* is a long vowel sound.
- In the word *hello*, / hel-lo / the first vowel *e* has a *short vowel sound,* and the *o* has a *long vowel sound.*

Even though they seldom appear in the English language outside of the dictionary, be sure you can tell the difference between the marks for short and long vowels. You might want to copy easy words from a dictionary, making the correct diacritical marks, for practice.

Additional Learning Activities

Review the rules for using vowels.

- When you see an *o* at the end of a word, the *o* has a long sound: *go, no, so,* and *yo-yo.*
- When *y* is acting like a vowel instead of a consonant: at the end of a word that has no other vowel, the *y* sounds like a long *I* as in *sky, try,* or *my.*
- When *y* is acting like a vowel at the end of a two-syllable word, the *y* sounds like a long *E* as in *city, hungry,* or *happy.*

Summary

Now let's see what we have learned about vowels. In the following words, underline each long vowel that says its name.

- smile, joke, fade, grape, use, him, over, under, man, bell, hello, only

Place the correct diacritical mark for each vowel in the preceding list.

CSML-016: VOWEL TEAMS

Systemic Phonics Sequence 10

Introduction

In many instances, vowel pairs are consistent with the first vowel being long and the second vowel being silent. But in a few cases, the first vowel is silent. Occasionally, the two vowels have a long sound or the vowel pair may have an entirely different sound.

Prerequisites for Learning

Before proceeding into (and beyond) this session, students should be familiar with the names and classifications (consonant or vowel) of all twenty-six letters and the primary sounds of the English alphabet *on sight*. This can be verified very quickly with an alphabet flash card set. Understanding the effect of context on the sound of a letter is highly desirable, but this may not be understood by early readers.

Why Do We Need to Know This?

Once again, the English language is so versatile that almost every letter is used to stand for several different sounds. These sounds depend on the other letters and sounds around the letter. It is especially true when working with long vowels. Just because the names of the long vowels are easy to master (their primary sounds are the same as the letter name) does not mean that they will always sound the same. As an example of this, take a look at the word *boat*. In this case, the second vowel is silent. If not, it would have to be pronounced as "boe-ate."

Learning Activities

When two vowels are together in a word, the first is usually long and the second is usually silent.

Boat: A single-syllable word in which the first vowel *o* is long and the second vowel "*a*" is silent.

- **Team**: A single-syllable word in which the first vowel "*e*" is long and the second vowel "*a*" is silent.
- **Tail**: A single-syllable word in which the first vowel "*a*" is long and the second vowel "*i*" is silent.
- **Seat**: A single-syllable word in which the first vowel "*e*" is long and the second vowel "*a*" is silent.
- **Feet**: A single-syllable word in which the first vowel "*e*" is long and the second vowel "*e*" is silent.
- **Coat**: A single-syllable word in which the first vowel *o* is long and the second vowel *a* is silent.

Helpful Hint for Learners

"When two vowels go walking, the front [first] one does the talking." Learn the consistent words—the ones that follow the rule—first. Then look for exceptions, particularly when the first vowel is followed by *u*, *o*, or *i* (good, spoon, broom, proof, proud, loud, cloud, etc.).

The *ai* and *ay* Vowel Teams

In both of these teams, the *a* is usually long and the second vowel is silent.

- *ai*: tail, mail, fail, rail, pail, wait

- *ay*: pay, stay, play, clay, okay

The *au* and *aw* Vowel Teams

In both of these teams, the sound is referred to as a *broad a* sound as heard in the words ball, fall, and tall. The sound occurs when the *a* is followed by a double l (*ll*).

- *au* is usually located in the beginning (*au*to) or in the middle (t*au*ght) of a word.
- *aw* comes at the end in most cases (dr*aw*, s*aw*, j*aw*, and str*aw*) except in the case of words like *aw*e, *aw*ful, *aw*esome, or p*aw*.

The *ee, ey,* and *ea* Vowel Teams

In each of these teams, the *e* is usually long, and the second vowel is silent.

- ee: bee, cheek, sleep, etc.
- ey: either a long *e* sound (key, honey, etc.) or a long *a* sound (they, obey, etc.)
- ea: eat, easy, beat, feat, etc.

The *oa* Vowel Team

This vowel team has a regular sound. In most cases, the *o* is usually long, and the second vowel *a* is silent.

- boat, coat, goat, road, etc.

The *ei* and *ie* Vowel Teams

The most common sound for *ei* is the long *e*.

- receive, either, and ceiling, etc.

The *ei* team can have three sounds: a *long a* in words like *weight* or *rein*, a *long i* when it comes at the end of a smaller word such as *cries* or *fried*, or it can sound like a *long e* as in *brief* or *believe*.

Helpful Hint for Learners

There is also a spelling rule for the *ie/ei* vowel team: *I* before *e* except after *c*.

The *ue*, *ui*, and *ew* Vowel Teams

In all these teams, the most common sound is like *oo* in the word food.

- blue, fruit, bruise, glue, grew, true, stew, flew

Practice Activities

Copy and pronounce the following double-vowel words onto a piece of paper or a word list. Then underline the vowel team in each of the words.

- nail, mail, week, load, beat, beet, foam, chair, team, deal, eat, load, seen, oak

Example: *Coat*: A single syllable word in which the first vowel *o* is long, and the second vowel *a* is silent.

Additional Learning Activities

Look for double-vowel vowel team words in a variety of printed materials. Any age-appropriate reading materials will provide you with a wealth of opportunities to find new words and learn more about the world.

One feature we are particularly fond of is "It Pays to Increase Your Word Power" which is published monthly in *Reader's Digest*. Use this to really sharpen your reading and pronunciation skills—and you will add at least twenty new words to your personal vocabulary every month.

Another interesting pastime is playing Scrabble with your friends. You might even want to try word searches or crossword puzzles—they all are designed to challenge you and help you constantly learn new things. When Rita was growing up, her whole family gathered around the dinner table to play Scrabble and other word games. She credits "It Pays to Increase Your Word Power" as one of the formative experiences leading her to become an English Major and career educator.

Summary

We are only four sections away from the end of our phonics elements. Now would be a good time to review how far we have come from just learning the alphabet.

1. Systematic Phonics Sequence
2. Sounding Out Letters
3. Additional New Sounds and Letters
4. Consonants That Sound the Same
5. Remaining Single Consonants
6. Consonant Blends
7. Consonant Digraphs
8. Short Vowels
9. Long Vowels
10. Vowel Teams

And one final thought to share with students as we move on from here. "You are gaining one of the most valuable things you will ever have. It's something you always have with you, something you won't ever lose, something no one can take away from you, something that will never break or wear out, and something you can use to change your life. What do you think that thing might be?"

CSML-017: THE SPECIAL E

Systematic Phonics Sequence 11

Introduction

In words containing two vowels, one of which is a final *e* at the end of the word, the first vowel is long and the final *e* is silent. Examples of this are *made*, *kite*, and *cape*.

Prerequisites for Learning

At this point, students should be capable of recognizing and reciting the alphabet and be aware that there are more than twenty-six sounds associated with the twenty-six letters in the alphabet. According to linguistic experts, there are forty-five common sounds. Ideally, students should also have developed a sight-word resource of nearly a thousand words, many of which are *expendables* with some phonic variations (*i.e., cap, cape, escape, escaped, ow, owl, row, crow, throw*).

Why Do We Need to Know This?

As students become more capable in a language, they become more able to express themselves in a variety of situations. They can also better understand what others are saying. With these widening abilities, they are ready to focus their language and provide more concise definitions of the world around them.

The "dream" goal should be to command a *fluent* spoken and written vocabulary of between six thousand and ten thousand words. One of the ways emerging readers can accomplish this is by mastering the simple rules of the Special E.

Learning Activities

In many ways, the Special E is the easiest of the phonic elements to learn the rule, which you see under the *helpful hint for learners* heading. But one other thing to notice is there is no relationship between the original word and the word created by the Special E.

Pronounce the following sets of Special E words:

Dim = dime	Cut = cute	Pal = pale	Pet = Pete
Rip = ripe	Kit = kite	Fin = fine	Can = cane

Helpful Hint for Learners

"*E* on the end makes the first vowel long, and the *e* is always silent."

Additional Learning Activities

Notice that even the short *e* in / *pet = Pete* / becomes long when there is an *e* at the end of the word.

Open a book or any other full page of words. Count (or mark using a highlighter) all the Special E words you find. (*Time* was *Tim. Mare* was *mar. Fare* was *far.*)

Summary

The Special E is simple to learn, simple to use, and works in almost any word, but there are exceptions to the rule … *simple* is one of those exceptions. I am pointing this out to reinforce the idea that in pronouncing any word, apply the rule first—and if it doesn't sound right, try other sounds until one fits.

CSML-018: R-CONTROLLED VOWELS

Systematic Phonics Sequence 12

Introduction

When single vowels are followed by the letter *r*, their sound is changed. It becomes a blended sound which isn't long or short but is a new sound. *R*-controlled vowels are also called *vowel plus r* or *Bossy R*.

Diacritical marks for *r*-controlled vowels look like two dots over the initial vowel sound. In a dictionary, you will notice these dots placed over the initial vowel sound, over the *a, e, i, o,* or *u.*

- a+r = *ar,* as in c*ar*
- e+r = er, as in h*er*
- i+r = *ir,* as in f*ir*st
- o+r = *or,* as in f*or*
- u+r = *ur,* as in f*ur*

Prerequisites for Learning

As is the case with all the advanced rules of reading and speaking, students should recognize, recite the alphabet, and be aware that there are more than twenty-six sounds associated with the twenty-six letters in the alphabet. According to linguistic experts, there are forty-five common sounds. The student should also be familiar with consonant blends, digraphs, and vowel teams, as well as the controlling function of the Special E.

A short review exercise covering these elements would be appropriate to begin this session.

Why Do We Need to Know This?

Knowing the *proper* pronunciation of a number of words is viewed as one important characteristic of language fluency. The most difficult part of this is mastering the exceptions to the general rules that govern special cases of pronunciation.

Learning Activities

When single vowels are followed by the letter *r*, their sound is changed. It becomes a blended sound—not long or short but a new sound. An *r* that controls vowels (*vowel + r*) is also referred to as a *Bossy R*.

A dictionary's diacritical marks for *r*-controlled vowels look like two dots over the initial vowel sound. In a dictionary, you notice these dots placed over the initial vowel sound, over the *a, e, i, o,* or *u*.

- a+r = *ar*, as in c*ar*
- e+r = er, as in h*er*
- i+r = *ir*, as in f*ir*st
- o+r = *or*, as in f*or*
- u+r = *ur*, as in f*ur*

Helpful Hint for Learners

The Bossy R is a "special case" pronunciation that only affects five specific spelling/pronunciation conditions, but they apply in almost every occurrence.

Additional Learning Activities

Practice the rule "vowel sounds are different when they precede an *r*."

- *ar:* part, park, star, start, car, mark, chart, march, far, hard, bark, barn

- *er:* term, her, germ, clerk, teacher, fern, master, toaster, further, hamster
- *ir:* stir, dirt, sir, birth, twirl, shirt, bird, flirt, girl, third
- *or:* corn, or, nor, for, cork, sport, fork, short, torn, north, corn
- *ur:* curl, curve, spur, spurt, fur, furniture, burn, turn

Find as many r-controlled vowels as possible in written materials. Record these words on paper or put them up on index cards for your word wall.

Fold a sheet of paper (lengthwise) into five columns. Head each of these columns with one of the Bossy R vowel-consonant combinations: *AR, ER, IR, OR,* or *UR.* Then, in each column, list as many of each word type as possible. Set a time limit (usually five to ten minutes). Make sure the words are correctly spelled and pronounced.

Summary

Like the Special E, the r-controlled vowel is easy to learn, simple to use, and works with almost any word, but there are exceptions to the rule. Once you have mastered the concept, it is time to notice exceptions.

The best way to build your vocabulary of r-controlled sight words is to keep adding them to your flash cards and going over them at least once a week.

CSML-019: DIPHTHONGS

Systematic Phonics Sequence 13

Introduction

Usually, when two vowels are together, the first one is long and the second is silent—as with vowel teams. There are, however, other interesting vowel combinations called *diphthongs*. These include *oi, ou, oo,* and *oy*. Vowel digraphs or teams are similar (*au, aw, eu,* and *ew*). The combinations *eu* and *ew* are often pronounced like a long '*u*' (as in *feud*) or as *oo* (as in *moon*).

Prerequisites for Learning

As in the cases of the Special E and r-controlled vowels, students should recognize, recite the alphabet, and know that there are more than twenty-six sounds associated with the twenty-six letters in the alphabet. According to linguistic experts, there are forty-five common sounds. The student should also be familiar with consonant blends, digraphs, and vowel teams, as well as the controlling function of the Special E.

A short review exercise covering these elements would be appropriate to begin this session.

Why Do We Need to Know This?

Diphthongs will give you an easier and more consistent way to learn the *proper* pronunciation of a number of words.

Learning Activities

Diphthongs are said to be "whiners and screamers." A teacher in Arizona said, "*Au* and *aw* are sad sounds. *Ew, ou, ow,* and *oo* are stinky sounds. *Oi, oy,* and *ow,* are ouchy, pinchy sounds."

Have fun making exaggerated sounds for diphthongs. There are no diacritical markings for these sounds.

There are, of course, exceptions to the rule. While the sound for *ow* is usually as it is heard in words such as *vowel* and *towel*, it can have the long *o* sound in *bow, bowl, tow, row, slow,* or *below.*

Helpful Hint for Learners

When practicing reading, always pronounce the word to yourself to hear the more comfortable sound in the context. Then, if there is still any doubt, check a dictionary for both pronunciation and meaning.

Additional Learning Activities

Begin practicing with this Easy-Start diphthong list:

- *down, cowboy, plow, how, now cow, found, out, boy, toy, boil, enjoy, smooth, roof, foil, shout, pout, aloud, round, count, join, choose, boot, ouch, broil, noise, house, grouch, bloom, igloo, cloud, loud, vowel*

Look for diphthongs in written materials, noticing any vowel digraphs such as *jaw, raw,* and *thaw.* Be sure to practice new words as sight words.

Using a column method, list vowel diphthongs and digraphs, and place as many words of each type in every column. Set a time limit (usually five or ten minutes). As usual, make sure the words are correctly spelled and pronounced.

Summary

Like Special E and r-controlled vowels, diphthongs are simple to learn, easy to use, and work in almost any word, but there are exceptions to the rule. Once you have mastered the concept, it is the time to notice exceptions.

The best way to build your vocabulary of diphthong sight words is to keep adding them to your flash cards and going over them at least once a week.

CSML-020: REMAINING SPECIAL SOUNDS

Systematic Phonics Sequence 14

Introduction

Another common vowel sound is heard in the unaccented syllable of words with more than one syllable. It is an "un-sound" or *schwa*, like *uh*. The dictionary diacritical marking looks like an upside-down e. Examples of this are found in words like el*e*phant (el-*uh*-fant), bac*o*n (bac-*uh*n), or min*u*s (min-*uh*s).

Prerequisites for Learning

As is the case with the Special E and r-controlled vowels, students should be able to recognize, recite the alphabet, and be aware that there are more than twenty-six sounds associated with the twenty-six letters in the alphabet. According to linguistic experts, there are forty-five common sounds. The student should also be familiar with consonant blends, digraphs, and vowel teams, as well as the controlling function of the Special E.

A short review exercise covering these elements would be appropriate to begin this session.

Why Do We Need to Know This?

These remaining special sounds are, basically, minor elements that can make a great difference in your spoken language. In some cases, they appear to be exceptions to the rule, but if they are ignored, they make your speech sound strange, if not foreign. Take, for example, what would happen to elephant (el-*uh*-fant) using "normal" rules: it would likely be pronounced as el-e-fant with a long *e* somewhere in the mix or like someone's initials (L. F. Ant).

Learning Activities

As you read in the introduction, a common semi-vowel sound is heard in the unaccented syllable of words having more than one syllable. It is an "un-sound" or *schwa*, like *uh*. The dictionary diacritical marking looks like an upside-down e. Examples of this are found in words like elephant (el-*uh*-fant), bacon (bac-*uh*n), or minus (min-*uh*s).

You can treat the schwa as a kind of exception or simply ignore it as a special function. When it shows up in a word simply think, *That's an exception.*

There are two other special vowel combinations: *ia* and *io*. When either of these is preceded by a *c, s,* or *t,* the combinations have either an *sh* or *zh* sound (and you just passed one example in the word combination where *tion* is pronounced like *shun*).

Other examples are seen in words such as television, station, action, vision, and social.

Summary

We have now covered most of the elements of phonics, but always remember that while phonics is a marvelous way to learn about a language, it does not tell you everything. Knowing the word only counts when you also know how it is properly spelled—and you know what it means in context.

Always keep an eye out for exceptions to the rule, and never use English phonics to try learning another language.

CSML-021: ANALYZING WORD PARTS

Introduction to Structural Analysis

Introduction

Besides sounding out words, another way to decode or recognize new words is by taking them apart. This process is known as structural analysis and includes recognizing word families, compound words, roots, prefixes, suffixes, contractions, syllables, and the plural and possessive word forms. The next six mini lessons each deal with one of the above structures.

This page serves only to introduce the concept of structural analysis and as a comprehensive index to the six elements listed above.

There is a seventh element, context, which is not dealt with in this section because it deals primarily with the definition of a word within a sentence rather than with the structure of the word itself.

Related Mini Lessons and Additional Reading on This Subject

- CSML-022: Word Families (phonograms or rhyming words)
- CSML-023: Compound Words (words formed by combining two words)

- CSML-024: Roots, Prefixes, and Suffixes (building new words from a single word and adding affixes)
- CSML-025: Contractions (combining two words into one by omitting letters and replacing them with an apostrophe)
- CSML-026: Syllabication (breaking words apart into their phonemic parts)
- CSML-027: Plurals and Possessives (identifying whether a word means *more than one* (plural) or *belonging to or owned by* (possessive).

CSML-022: WORD FAMILIES

Structural Analysis 1

Introduction

Working with word families is a fun, joyous experience. It is so easy to make new words from these basic patterns included below. About fifty (most common) word families make up more than five hundred English words! Using the patterns listed in this section provides practice for forming countless new words.

Sometimes word families are called *phonograms* or rhyming words. In building these words, the beginning is called the *onset* and the rhyming pattern is called the *rime*.

Prerequisites for Learning

Students should recognize, recite the alphabet, and be aware that there are more than twenty-six sounds associated with the twenty-six letters in the alphabet. According to most linguistic experts, there are forty-five common sounds. The student also should be familiar with consonant blends, digraphs, and vowel teams as well as the controlling function of the Special E.

Why Do We Need to Know This?

We are now in the stage of English language development and literacy where it is desirable to expand both the size and usefulness of your vocabulary. It is also a time when the language can be an invaluable tool and a mental toy to play with.

Being familiar with word families makes it much easier to increase both reading rate and comprehension.

Remember that the *onset* is the letter or letter cluster that precedes the vowel in a one-syllable word, and in all cases the *rime* is the vowel and any following consonants at the end of the word. Usually the rime is the rhyming segment of the word. The capability to understand and use onsets and rimes helps spelling and word recognition/identification.

Learning Activities

Repeating what was said in the introduction to this CSML, approximately fifty word families make up more than five hundred English words. Using the patterns listed in this section allows them to be used to form a multitude of words.

Sometimes word families are called phonograms or rhyming words. In building these words, the beginning is called the onset, and the rhyming pattern is called the rime.

It is easy to see why these fifty rhyming patterns are easy to learn and use:

ack	ag	ain	ake	all	am	ame	an	and	ap
ar	at	ate	ay	ead	ed	ee	eed	eet	ell
en	ent	et	ice	ig	ight	ill	in	ine	ing
ink	ip	it	ite	oak	ock	od	ode	og	oon
op	ot	ouse	ub	ug	ump	un	up	ut	y

Figure 22-1: Fifty Common Rhyming Patterns

So many words are made up of these patterns that these become instantly recognized words.

Helpful Hint for Learners

Learn or review at least one or two patterns a day. Start by building a list of "quick" words by writing the individual pattern on a sheet of lined paper and then adding consonants in front of that pattern. Put an X where the onset does not make up a word.

Example: Onset = [ ], Rime = 'an'

(An X indicates no common word is formed using this exercise.)

[a] + an = X	[b] + an = ban	[c] + an = can	[d] + an = Dan
[e] + an = X	[f] + an = fan	[g] + an = X	[h] + an = X
[i] + an = Ian	[j] + an = Jan	[k] + an = X	[l] + an = X
[m] + an = man	[n] + an = Nan	[o] + an = X	[p] + an = pan
[q] + an = X	[r] + an = ran	[s] + an = X	[t] + an = tan
[u] + an = X	[v] + an = van	[w] + an = wan	[x] + an = X
[y] + an = X	[z] + an = X		

By now, you should have noticed that, as general rules: 1) all the rhyming patterns begin with a vowel, and 2) none of the rhyming patterns are preceded by another vowel to form words.

Additional Learning Activities

As you complete the instructional hint for each of the fifty rhyming patterns, start building more words when you read through paragraphs, exercises, or other texts. For example:

- Pattern *an*: beg*an*, br*an*, sp*an*, pl*an*, etc.

Look for word families in written materials; also, be sure to practice new words as sight words.

Use word families to identify rhyming words. Identify all the words in the word family on one or two printed pages, and then see if you can build rhyming verses using these words at the end of short sentences.

Summary

The best way to start building your vocabulary of word families is to locate them in your collection of sight words. Add them if they are not part of it already. Remember that you are not only learning how to work with the language but you should also be finding ways to play with it.

In a way, building a vocabulary can be like building a stamp collection, or a collection of baseball cards, leaves, or rocks. Gather what words you want (or need) to accomplish your goals. If you think about it, you can even build your own games with friends and enjoy hours upon hours of constructive play.

CSML-023: COMPOUND WORDS

Structural Analysis 2

Introduction

Compound words are two words that are put together to form a new word. These are side-by-side words. To remember what they are, simply say, "You take two words and squash them together."

Starting with concrete objects or drawing compound word parts, check out basic compound words. Be sure spelling and pronunciation for the new words are accurate. Begin with more concrete words before you move to abstract ones. It is easier to learn the word *eyelash* than the word *afternoon*.

Prerequisites for Learning

Students should recognize and recite the alphabet and be aware that there are more than twenty-six sounds associated with the twenty-six letters in the alphabet. According to linguistic experts, there are forty-five common sounds. The student also should be familiar with consonant blends, digraphs, and vowel teams as well as the controlling function of the Special E.

Why Do We Need to Know This?

We are now in the stage of English language development and literacy where it is desirable to expand both the size and usefulness of the vocabulary. It is also a time when the language can begin to be seen as both an invaluable tool and a mental toy.

Being familiar with compound words makes it much easier to increase both reading rate and comprehension.

Learning Activities

As we said in the introduction, compound words are two words that are put together to form a new word. These are side-by-side words. To remember what they are, simply remember to say, "You take two words and squash them together." You might also think of them as "sardines in a can" providing a useful result.

Begin with this Easy-Start list of compound words. Underline the two words that make up the compound word or place a dividing line (/) between the two words.

- farmhouse, cowgirl, newspaper, grandchild, moonlight
- nightgown, mailman, sunshine, airplane, handbag
- schoolroom, birthday, highway, sailboat

Use this list of compound words and draw a line to divide the two words that make up the compound word.

- farm / house, cow / girl, news / paper, grand / child
- moon / light, night / gown, mail / man, sun / shine
- air / plane, hand / bag, school / room, birth / day
- high / way, sail / boat

Helpful Hint for Learners

Compound words are not the same as hyphenated terms. A grey-green coat cannot be compressed into a compound word. As a general rule, compound words are used as nouns, and hyphenated terms are used as adjectives or adverbs.

Additional Learning Activities

Find as many compound words as possible on one page of a newspaper. Using colored pencils or markers, underline, circle, or put a triangle around each word.

Find compound words in a variety of written materials. Keep a list of compound words on notecards, in word rings, or on your word wall.

Summary

The best way to continue building your vocabulary with compound words is to locate them in your collection of sight words or add them if they are not part of it already. Remember that you are not only learning how to work with the language but you should also be finding ways to play with it.

Note to Coaches

This can be done as an individual exercise or as a fun team contest. Each "contestant" (individual or team) is given the same page from a newspaper. Then each is given a specified time to go over that page to locate as many compound words (hyphenated words can be done as a game alternative) as possible. In some cases, it might be best to use this following CSML-026 (Syllabication) to demonstrate the difference between hyphenated words and word hyphenation, which is actually a text-structural element.

In a way, building a vocabulary can be like building a stamp collection, or a collection of baseball cards, leaves, or rocks. In each of these activities, you gather what words—or other specific items—you want (or need) to accomplish your goals.

Once this mini lesson in completed, increased understanding of the structure and development of compound words can actually take place unconsciously by using reader-made sight-reading cards. Simply write the individual component words on the first line of an index card and the compound word on the second line. If you want to improve the usefulness of these cards, you can add a definition and other grammar-related information at the bottom of the card.

school + room =

schoolroom

Also see synonym: "classroom"

*A room, usually located at a school,
specific to learning activities*

Figure 23-1: Sample Word Wall Sight Learning Card

CSML-024: AFFIXES, PREFIXES, AND SUFFIXES

Structural Analysis 3

Introduction

Affixes are sort of like train cars. Sometimes, they are in front of the engine (which we call the root word). We call these prefixes. Sometimes they follow it. We call these suffixes. The word *affix* means to connect or add on, which is what we are doing when we take a syllable and add it on to the front of a root word.

The word syllable *pre* comes from Latin and means "to go before." So when we add the syllable *pre* to the word *fix*, it becomes a prefix (something added before a word to create a new word with a new meaning).

A suffix is exactly the opposite. It is a *fix* that follows the root word to create a new word with a new meaning.

Prerequisites for Learning

Prefixes and suffixes are learned as distinct units that are visually separated from the rest of the word. Students at this point need a good foundation in all the fundamental English language elements. This means they need to be familiar with all the elements presented in sections CSML-003 through CSML-023.

Why Do We Need to Know This?

We are now in the stage of English language development and literacy where it is desirable to expand both the size and usefulness of the vocabulary. It is also a time when the language can begin to be seen as both an invaluable tool and a mental toy.

An understanding of the form and function of affixes, prefixes, and suffixes makes it possible to create and understand a number of words—with many different functions and meanings—from a single word.

Learning Activities

To review, as stated in the introduction, affixes are sort of like train cars. Sometimes, they are in front of the engine (which we call the root word). We call these prefixes. Sometimes they follow it. We call these suffixes. The word *affix* means to connect or add on, which is what we are doing when we take a syllable and add it on to the front of a root word.

The word syllable *pre* comes from Latin and means "to go before." So when we add the syllable *pre* to the word *fix,* it becomes a *prefix* (something added before a word to create a new word with a new meaning).

A *suffix* is exactly the opposite. It is a *fix* that follows the root word to create a new word with a new meaning.

There is another *-fix* category, called an *in-fix*. It means a situation in which a word is divided at a syllable break (or between two related words) and an expressive word is inserted into the middle. There are few places where this is used appropriately, and it is mentioned only to identify it in those rare occasions.

Affixes are not the same as compound words. Both prefixes and suffixes usually modify the meaning of words and often can change the part of speech, as in the use of *s, es, ed, ing, ly,* and *y.* One thing to be careful of, in building suffixes, they may cause the spelling of the root word to change. For example, the root word *easy* becomes *easily,* or *day* becomes *daily.*

Prefixes and suffixes are best learned by rote (memorization) with examples. At a minimum, be sure to learn the following most well-known examples.

The most common prefixes are: *re, in, con, de, dis, com, un, ex, pro, pre,* and *en*. The prefixes *pre* and *per* are often confused; *per* means *through* or *as a result of*, and *pre* means *before* or *in front of*.

Common suffixes include: *ly, er, est, tion, ness, ful, any, ous, ious, ent,* and *ment.*

Helpful Hint for Learners

- Affixes usually form separate syllables.
- Affixes are not the same as compound words. Both prefixes and suffixes usually modify the meaning of words and often can change the part of speech.
- They can also do a lot to build your score when playing Scrabble!
- Just like a train, prefixes and suffixes can be "chained" to create more words. For example, the root word *able* can become *dis*able and then disabl*ing*.
- Have fun with this long, interesting word chain. People often have fun looking them up in the dictionary, saying, and spelling them.
- *Antidisestablishmentarianism* = anti [p] dis [p] establish [r] ment [s] arian [s] ism [s].

Additional Learning Activities

Here are some prefix and suffix words to play with:

- *re*: redo, relearn, replace
- *in:* indoor, inland (Words such as insert or intent are not prefixes. They are most commonly used as roots [r] with a prefix such as reinsert or a suffix as insertion or intention.)
- *dis*: disagree, dislike, distrust
- *un*: unsure, unwashed, undress, uncover
- *ful*: skillful, peaceful, joyful, cheerful

Another good way to learn a new word is to recognize the root word. Roots are base words that make up the English language. Root words are usually words made up of one or two syllables that provide basic meaning.

Review root words and their variants—including the various endings—to indicate tense (*rush/rushed*), number (*girl/girls*), or comparative relationship (*er/est*).

Prefixes and suffixes represent meaning components.

Summary

Using lists and affixes excerpted from *Reading Champions!* (See figures 24-1 and 24-2) or words from other texts, practice identifying some of these basic prefixes and suffixes. Make sure the meanings are understood as well as the process for applying the meaning of the affix. Words need to be spelled correctly.

EASY START PREFIX LIST

PREFIX	MEANING	EXAMPLE
ante	before	antebellum (before a war),
anti	against	antibiotic, antivenom, antiseptic
auto	self	autobiography
bi	two	bicycle, bifocal
cent	hundred; 1/100	centigrade; centipede
deci	ten; 1/10	decimal
dis	not; opposite	disagree; dishonest
in	not	inaccurate, inactive
im	not	immature, impossible
mal	bad	malfunction
milli	thousand; 1/1000	millimeter; millisecond
mis	bad; opposite	misbehave; misalign;
multi	many	multicolored; multimillionaire
oct	eight	octopus; octagon
off	from	offstage
on	on	ongoing, onshore
over	above; too much	overpriced; overdo; overdone
para	beside	parallel; paraphrase
peri	around	periscope, perimeter
post	after	postdate, postpone, postscript
pre	before	precaution, preamble, preview
pro	for; in favor or	protagonist
re	do again	redo, rewrite, reappear
sub	under, lesser, beneath	submarine, subliminal, subsidiary
super	over; above; extreme	supervisor, superabundant
tri	three	tricycle, triangle
uni	one; single	unicorn, unicycle
under	below; below average	underweight, understated, underpass
un	not	unhappy

Figure 24-1: Easy-Start Prefix List

EASY START SUFFIX LIST

PREFIX	MEANING	EXAMPLE
~able (also ~ible)	capable	teachable, buildable
~age	action; process	marriage, voyage
~ant	one who	assistant
~ar	one who	liar
~arian	one who specializes	librarian, historian
~cle	small	icicle, particle
~cule	tiny	molecule
~ectomy	surgical removal	tonsillectomy
~er (also ~r; ~or)	one who does	baker, teacher, actor, doctor
~ery (also ~ry)	performance of work	bakery, dentistry
~hood	state; quality;	neighborhood, likelihood
~ing	material; purpose	frosting, bedding
~itis	inflammation	laryngitis, arthritis
~man	occupation	mailman, fireman
~ment	an object	instrument, ornament
~ment	state; quality; condition	amusement, puzzlement
~less	lacking	friendless, childless
~ling	comparison or identity	duckling, weakling, changeling
~ship	condition; related to	friendship, apprenticeship, woodsmanship
~er	comparative status	smaller, taller, wider, inner, outer, upper
~ine	chemical compound	chlorine, caffeine, turpentine
~ful	fullness	wonderful, thoughtful
~ness	quality	happiness, kindness, wilderness
~ology	science of; study of	Biology, Geology, Ecology,
~s (also ~es)	plural	toys, foxes, trees, movements
~phobia	fear of	claustrophobia, agoraphobia
~ern	general direction	northern, southern, southwestern
~th	state; condition; quality	warmth, strength, length

Figure 24-2: Easy-Start Suffix List

CSML-025: CONTRACTIONS

Structural Analysis 4

Introduction

Structural analysis helps us take apart the structure of our language. After mastering basic phonics, learning the backbone of the language makes it easier to teach reading. Contractions are a major part of the structure of our language. Contractions make our language clear and concise and are a lot of fun to teach to new and emerging readers.

A contraction is a short form of two words. The words are put together (sort of like a compound word), and then one or more letters are removed and replaced by an apostrophe.

- *We are* becomes *weare*, then the *a* is removed and replaced by the apostrophe ('), which leaves us with the contraction *we're*.
- *She is* becomes *sheis*, then the *i* is removed and replaced by an apostrophe ('), which leaves us with the contraction *she's*.

It's just that simple! *Don't* you agree? (Be careful with this one because *its* is the possessive of *it*.)

Prerequisites for Learning

Prefixes and suffixes are learned as distinct units separated from the rest of the word. Students at this point need a good foundation in all the English language fundamentals. This means they need to be familiar with all the elements presented in sections CSML-003 through CSML-020.

Why Do We Need to Know This?

We are now in the stage of English language development and literacy where it is desirable to streamline the vocabulary.

Understanding the process of creating contractions makes it possible to apply a number of words in order to combine related smaller words to express ourselves.

Learning Activities

Remember, a contraction is a short form of two words. When one or more letters are removed and replaced by an apostrophe, this is basically like contracting something from something. "You take the letter out and then put the apostrophe in." Here are a few other examples:

- *I am* becomes *Iam*, and then the *a* is removed and replaced by the apostrophe ('), which leaves us with the contraction *I'm*.
- *You are* becomes *youare*, and then the *a* is removed and replaced by an apostrophe, leaving us with the contraction *you're*.
- *We are* changes to *weare*, and then changes to *we're*.

Now let's model the contraction process.

- is not = isnot = isn't
- I am = Iam = I'm
- he is = heis = he's
- we are = weare = we're.

Helpful Hint for Learners

"You take the letter out and put the apostrophe in!" You can chant this and use your hands to model it. Both coach and learner can do it with exaggerated hand motions, for every contraction you practice.

Additional Learning Activities

Here are some common contractions to review the process, but this time, remove the apostrophe, insert the missing letter and the space, and write the two original words.

Example: aren't = are not

can't = ____ ____	couldn't = ____ ____
didn't = ____ ____	doesn't = ____ ____
hadn't = ____ ____	hasn't = ____ ____
haven't = ____ ____	isn't = ____ ____
wasn't = ____ ____	weren't = ____ ____
we'd = ____ ____	he'd = ____ ____
I'd = ____ ____	she'd = ____ ____
they'd = ____ ____	we'd = ____ ____
you'd = ____ ____	he'll = ____ ____
I'll = ____ ____	it'll = ____ ____
she'll = ____ ____	there'll = ____ ____
we'll = ____ ____	they're = ____ ____
we're = ____ ____	you're = ____ ____
we've = ____ ____	you've = ____ ____
I'm = ____ ____	he's = ____ ____
here's = ____ ____	it's = ____ ____

Figure 25-1: Contractions Exercise

There are exceptions, such as *won't* (will not) or *can't* (can not) where the Easy-Start rule does not apply. If these come up, simply say, "This is an exception," but understand that the rule does apply in a vast majority of situations.

Using the above list, make sure all regular contractions are recognized and understood. Find additional contractions in other written materials. Also make lists of contractions and make flash cards, word rings, etc.

Summary

Make sure the meanings of all contractions are understood as well as the process for creating and breaking them. Also make sure that words are spelled correctly.

Special Note

There is a detailed process/procedure for creating contractions, abbreviations, etc. provided in the Government Printing Office (GPO) Style Guide. This publication, available from the US Government Printing Office, has proven an invaluable resource for writers for the past fifty years.

CSML-026: SYLLABICATION

Structural Analysis 5

Introduction

A syllable is part of a word. As a matter of fact, in some cases a syllable *is* the word (like *A* or *I*). But usually a syllable (word part) is made up of a vowel sound and one or more consonants. Then each word is made up of one or more syllables.

And once you have all this information down pat, you also have another tool for figuring out the sounds of new and longer words. That tool is called syllabication, or simply breaking a word down into its smaller components.

In this case, it means breaking a word down into three syllables.

- Syllab ("shortened" form for syllab~~le~~)
- + ic (which means *pertaining to* … in this case, syllab~~le~~) = syllabic
- + ation (performing an action) = syllabication

Prerequisites for Learning

Prefixes and suffixes are learned as distinct units visually separated from the rest of the word. Students, at this point, need a good foundation in all the fundamental English language elements. Especially significant, prefixes and suffixes can be used to modify a root word or phrase to create new words.

Why Do We Need to Know This?

As we encounter new and longer words, we need a way to break them down into their components to extract their intended meanings. In CSML-024, we learned how to use prefixes and suffixes to build concise language used to clarify the meanings of our sentences. In this unit, we do exactly the opposite—break a word down into its components to extract the concise meaning.

Learning Activities

Every syllable (or word part) is made up of one vowel sound and one or more consonants. The key, here, is to remember that each syllable must have a vowel sound, each vowel sound identifies one syllable. It is also important to remember that vowel sounds can be represented by a single vowel (like the *i* in *it, if,* or *gift*), a vowel diphthong (like the *oo* in *moon*), or by a vowel pair (like the *ea* in *team*) where the first vowel is long and the second vowel is silent.

Learning to listen closely to a word and counting the number of vowel sounds will help you understand the number of syllables. Only vowel sounds count, however, and silent letters should be ignored. Remember, the special vowel combinations, such as *au, aw, ay, oy, oi, ow, ou, oo,* and *ee,* only count as one vowel sound.

The purpose of learning syllables is to shorten long words into simple elements. Frequently, budding readers panic when seeing a long word; knowing the *Easy-Start* rules can make the decoding process a snap!

Let's start with two definitions and three basic syllable rules.

1. Open syllables end with a vowel, and closed syllables end with a consonant.
2. When there is a vowel-consonant-consonant-vowel (vccw) pattern, divide the consonants between the consonants. Examples are les/son and num/ber.

3. When there is a vowel-consonant-vowel (vcv) pattern, the consonant is usually part of the first syllable if the vowel is short. Examples are: tax/i, mu/sic, si/lent.

4. When *le* is found at the end of a word longer than one syllable, the final consonant joins with the *le* to form the last syllable. Examples are: stum/ble, ta/ble.

Then let's review five other rules. In the examples provided, decide if the syllables are open or closed.

1. If only one vowel sound is heard in a word, that word is one syllable and cannot be further divided. Examples are *late* and *bee*.

2. In words where two vowel sounds can be heard, two consonants stand together, and there is a vowel sound on each side, divide between the consonants. An example is but/ter.

3. Prefixes or suffixes, generally, are their own syllable. Examples are un/happy, and re/do.

4. In a two-syllable word with a consonant between the vowels and the first vowel is short, usually the second vowel sound will begin the second syllable. Examples are ma/gic and tro/pic.

5. In words with two or more syllables, look for compound words and divide between the two words. Examples are cup/cake and snow/flake.

Helpful Hint for Learners

Stressing what was said earlier, in the "Learning Activities" paragraphs, the purpose of learning to work with syllables is to shorten long words into simple elements. Frequently, new readers panic when seeing a long word, but knowing the Easy-Start rules can make the decoding process a snap!

Additional Learning Activities

Allow about five minutes each for the following eight exercises.

1. Use *le* combinations to make complete words. Common *le* combinations are: *ble* (as in tum/*ble*), *cle* (as in bi/cy/*cle*), *dle* (as in fid/*dle*), *gle* (as in gig/*gle*), *tle* (as in tur/*tle*).

2. Divide a given list of words into syllables by drawing a dividing line between the syllable(s). Take the words from any age-appropriate reading materials.

3. Practice dividing a variety of useful prefix and suffix words.

4. Practice dividing two-syllable words that have an *ed* added to a word ending in a *t* or *d*. Examples are add/*ed*, test/*ed*, and light/*ed*.

5. Divide these two-syllable words: *enter, after, taller, copper, supper.*

6. Drill and practice with any of the above rules that have been missed.

7. Find words where *y* functions as a vowel and is its own syllable.

8. Review open and closed syllables: *open* syllables end with a vowel, and *closed* syllables end with a consonant. Find several examples of each.

Summary

Syllables can be very useful in working out the meaning of long or complex words. Also, understanding syllables is an important part of being able to break down a poetic line into its proper rhythm (referred to as *scansion*) and establish the place to properly hy/-/phen/-/ate a long word in a sentence.

We will get fur/-/ther in these func/-/tions in fu/-/ture ses/-/sions on the sub/-/ject of writ/-/ing, but for now, just go out and dis/-/man/-/tle a cou/-/ple doz/-en words!

CSML-027: PLURALS AND POSSESSIVES

Structural Analysis 6

Introduction

Students need quick and easy lessons for both possessives and plurals because these two language structures are easily confused or mixed up. Plurals mean more than one thing. Possessives show ownership.

The most common plurals in the English language are *s* and *es*. Examples are *one boy, three boys, one car, several cars, one dollar, ten dollars, one wish, three wishes, one bush, five bushes.*

For most singular words or names, the possessive is formed by adding an apostrophe (') followed by an *s*. For example, "If that dollar belongs to Jim, it is Jim's dollar." "This class meets every Tuesday. This Tuesday's class will be to study singular and plural word forms."

Throughout this CSML, we study the differences using comparisons and contrasts in each of the cases.

Prerequisites for Learning

Students need to know all basic elements of the English language, including the alphabet and consonant and vowel forms and sounds. General language structures need to be above the emergent level.

Why Do We Need to Know This?

Understanding the differences in singular and plural forms is an essential part of decoding and understanding a message in its proper context.

Learning Activities

To review, students need quick and easy lessons for both possessives and plurals because these two language structures are easily mixed up. Plurals mean more than one thing. Possessives show ownership.

Basic Rules for Possessives

Form the possessive of a singular name, add an apostrophe (') and an *s*. Examples are the *girl's* dress and *Juan's* car,

Form the possessive of a plural word ending in *s* or a singular word ending in *s* by adding an apostrophe (') after the *s*. Examples are the *girls'* dresses and the *team's* bus (if there is more than one team, it would be the teams' bus.)

Basic Rules for Plurals

Many, if not most, words go from singular to plural by assigning an *s* or *es*. Examples are *one cat/many cats* and *one wish/many wishes*.

There are exceptions to both of these rules to learn as they are found in your reading exercises. But here are a few of the exceptions dealing with plural forms. One example of an exception might be *wife / wives* where the *fe* changes to a *v* and then requires an *es*.

Singular Words ending in *s, z, ch,* or *sh* require an *es* to change from singular to plural (*circus/circuses, buzz/buzzes,* and *church/churches*).

For words ending with consonants before a *y,* change the *y* to *i* and add *es* (*lady/ladies* and *city/cities*).

Singular words ending in *o* require an *es* to change from singular to plural (*hero/heroes*).

Helpful Hint for Learners

If you are talking about one object or person, you are dealing in the singular.

- Joseph has a book. That book is Joseph's book. Martha has four books. These are Martha's four books.

If you are talking about more than one person, you are speaking in the plural.

- Three boys each have their own bicycles. Those are the three boys' bicycles.

If you can't decide if a word is plural or possessive, think how much sense it would make if you were to insert *of the* in front of it.

- My uncle's pen is on the desk. The pen is on the desk. The pen of my uncle is on the desk. *Pen* is the subject, and *of my uncle* is a phrase that modifies (describes ownership of) the pen.

Additional Learning Activities

As is the case with most language elements, the best way to gain proficiency in dealing with singulars, plurals, and possessives is to play with them. Make a table with a hundred nouns and use the three examples in the "Helpful Hints for Learners" section above to create sentences showing the nouns in their singular, plural, and possessive forms.

SINGULAR	(S) POSSESSIVE	PLURAL	(P) POSSESSIVE
animal	animal's	animals	animals'
an animal	an animal's cage	those animals	those animals' cages
friend	friend's	friends	friends'
my friend Bill	my friend Bill's jacket	many friends	my many friends' jackets

Figure 27-1: Examples of Plurals and Possessives

Notice that the structures of the sentences also change, especially when looking at the descriptive articles/adjectives. Often, when looking at a word, the context in which it is used will give you a clue as to its form.

(*It,* by the way, is an exception to several rules. Both the plural and the possessive are *its—with no apostrophe. It's* is the contraction of *it is.*)

These rules remain fairly constant until you get into more advanced language skills and are working with punctuation and the structural features of texts in CSML-040.

Summary

Acquiring fluency in a language is much easier than some people think. Practice, drill, and repetition are the best way to build language skills. This is because practice builds skills that are applied automatically, without any conscious thought.

Imagine two baseball players whose (plural possessive of *who*) skills need to be automatic! A pitcher thinks *curveball* and automatically shifts his grip on the ball so the ball will curve when it is pitched. A batter has less than a second to see the ball released, estimate its speed and probable trajectory, and bring the bat around in time to meet the incoming pitch.

CSML-028: ORIGINS OF WORDS

Structural Analysis 7

Author Note

Although an understanding of the origins of words in English is a part of "Structural Analysis" (which is why it is shown as #7), we have chosen to break it out from the "Structural Analysis" group. The underlying linguistic and multilanguage foundations—is better placed in an advanced language skills environment.

Introduction

You may have read somewhere that out of twenty thousand common English words, more than twelve thousand are based on Greek or Latin roots. Many English words also come from German, French, Spanish, and other contemporary languages, and a few come from Native American, African, Japanese, Chinese, and Indian languages.

As a common practice, many languages and cultures borrow words from one another. For example, the Japanese word for bread is *pan [pronounced pahn]*, which is the same as the Spanish. Both words come from the Latin *panis,* which came from Greek, and originally from the Sanskrit word that means *leaf.* So in addition to studying basic prefixes and suffixes, a student may want to seek out word origins through extensive dictionary use, hard copies, or online research.

At a minimum, origins of many common words, as well as technical terms, provide students with the opportunity to understand how many words are formed. So many English words come from Latin and Greek that when one learns one root word, he or she has the key to an entire word family sequence!

For example, the words *graph* and *graphic*—and the suffix *ography*—come to us from the Greek word *graphos*, which means *to write [down]* or to record, as in the case of the word biography, which is a construct from two Greek roots: *bio* (meaning life) and *graphos* (to write).

Want a fun-to-know technical example? Offset lithography (a kind of printing) comes from *litho* (Latin for *rock*) and *graphos*. Together, the words literally mean, "writing from a rock."

Coaching Note

Develop a personal "short list" of word origins and common words. Model (working with the student) the rules for using these words to identify the root words and then use prefixes and suffixes to construct additional words.

Prerequisites for Learning

By this point in the learning sequence, the alphabet, consonant and vowel forms and sounds, and general language structures all need to be above the emergent level. This applies especially to the English Language learner (ELL) whose pronunciation of both vowels and consonants may differ widely from native English speakers.

One example of this is the Hispanic *ll*, which is pronounced like an English *y*. La Jolla (a city whose name is directly derived from Spanish is correctly pronounced *la hoya*). A native Spanish speaker might (quite rightfully) try to pronounce the name of the *holly* bush as *hoy* (or hoy-y) because there is no convention for a *yy* combination in Spanish.

Often, the ability to pronounce an English word properly requires familiarity with the language conventions of the language of origins. For example, *let* in French is pronounced as *lay*. This often demands that the coach, teacher, and student learn them on the way to fluency.

Why Do We Need to Know This?

Understanding the origins of historic and "foreign" words and phrases enables the listener—and the reader—to more accurately understand what is being heard or read. It also provides the speaker and writer with a greater command of the English language.

And as a humorous aside, it can be used to *amaze* your friends, *confound* (go ahead, look it up in the dictionary) your family, and *dazzle* your students.

The word *money* comes to us from the Latin *moneta* by way of French (*moneie*) and Old Middle English (*moneye*). There are five root definitions in the English language.

Learning Activities

This unit is as much about history and broad linguistic conventions as it is about learning to listen, speak, read, and write in English.

Isn't it amazing that more than half of the words in the English language (over 70 percent) are ultimately rooted in Greek, Latin, Spanish, French (which are referred to as Romance languages), and German? The fundamentals of the language came from several Northern European tribes, most notably the Angles, Saxons, Picts, and Scots, which blended into a single (homogenous) language originally heavily influenced by Norman French.

Most of our scientific and mathematical terms are derived from—or are constructs of—the Greeks (who borrowed heavily from Egyptian, Persian, and Sanskrit). Most of the terms and phrases used in our legal system come to us from Latin—the first civilization to create an empire-wide code of laws. These terms come to us almost intact (insofar as the language is concerned) because of an almost unbroken chain from Rome through the Roman Catholic Church to British common law.

Because of these many common roots, a fairly large number of words—some with vastly different meanings and parts of speech, all with essentially the same spelling and word sound—are found in English: As an example, the word *court*:

- Court—\kort\ noun, often attributed [Middle English, from Old French, from Latin] cohort, cohors, enclosure, group, retinue, cohort. This word then offers five definitions as a noun and three more as a transitive verb.

Helpful Hint for Learners

There is a great deal of additional information about word origins found in most high school and advanced dictionaries. The important thing to remember at this point is that your main interest is how the word's origins might affect pronunciation.

Additional Learning Activities

This is ambitious, but go to twenty different pages in any dictionary and select four words from each page (you will have a total of eighty words). Note the English phonetic spelling and then notice the phonetic spellings of the word's origins. As an example:

- Cous•cous: kus-kus noun [French couscous, couscoussou, from Arabic kuskus, kuskucu] First known (recorded) use of this word in English was in 1759.

Summary

More advanced students can research origins of many common words (as well as many technical terms). This offers opportunities to understand how many words are constructed from a single historic or "foreign" root. So many English words come from Latin and Greek that when one learns one root word, he or she has the key to an entire word family sequence.

Finally, learning and expanding your vocabulary, and an understanding of how deeply our language is embedded in the same roots as many of the world's languages is worth the time and effort.

- The name used by the media for the CEO of a modern industrial empire—Czar—is an Anglicized form of the title of the Imperial Russian Empire ruler—the Tsar. This came from Caesar, the ruler of the Roman Empire.

CSML-029: USING A DICTIONARY

Vocabulary Development Skills 1

Author's Note

Most dictionaries contain a section in the front that explains its use and the symbols applying to each specific word. To someone who has never used a dictionary (and even to some who have), the amount of information and symbolic codes can be overwhelming. But once you get the hang of it, you will find it becomes the most useful book in your library. Online dictionary use needs to be taught, as well. Encourage your students to be regular dictionary users. Model it.

Introduction

Probably everyone knows that dictionaries offer a source of information about spelling, pronunciation, and meaning of words. These are the major uses of any dictionary. But did you know that a good dictionary tells the part of speech (*part of grammar skills*) of a word? It gives you the origin (or origins) of a word. In some cases, it offers a synonym (words which mean the same thing) or an antonym (words with an opposite meaning) for your word. Most of the publishing standards used in this unit are excerpted from the Collegiate Edition of *Merriam Webster's Deluxe Dictionary* published by *Reader's Digest*.

Prerequisites for Learning

Learning to use an English dictionary is possible at almost every age and language skill level of "emergent" and above. Knowledge of alphabetic sequences is also important as well as the ability to distinguish and understand letter and syllable sounds. Newer readers might use an elementary level dictionary to avoid frustration caused by the sheer size of a typical collegiate dictionary.

Why Do We Need to Know This?

When you learn to use a dictionary, you automatically learn and reinforce at least three major sub-skills:

Locating Words
- knowing alphabetic sequence
- determining what letters precede and follow a given letter
- alphabetizing words according to beginning two or three letters
- using guide words effectively
- knowing how to use a "thumb index"
- identifying the parts of speech

Pronunciation Skills
- using key words and *diacritical* markings (look it up)
- recognizing syllables
- using accent marks
- understanding the phonetic spelling

Definition Skills
- knowing multiple meanings of the same word
- understanding the definitions
- selecting the correct definition for the context

Learning Activities

Here are eight *Easy-Start* success tips for working with a dictionary.

1. *Every* defined word in *every* dictionary is organized alphabetically. Names and other proper nouns are capitalized. Most dictionaries use either a bullet [•] or a slash [/] to indicate syllable breaks. If a word-phrase is being defined, a space is left between the words. As examples *dining room, di•no•saur, din/ner.*
    o   heartache = heart•ache (single *compound* word, no space)
    o   heart attack *n.* (two words, no space)
    o   heart-attack *adj.* (two words, hyphenated).
2. **Guide words** help locate a word, telling where (on which page) it is located. Guide words are located at the top of each page. The word at the top-left of the page is the first word being defined, and the word at the top-right is the last word being defined on that page.
3. **Brackets** [] are after the word being defined, they hold unique information, such as the word's origins.
4. **Parenthesis** () follow the defined word and offer the word's pronunciation.
5. **Accent marks** show emphasis, stress, or loudness on the syllables.
6. **Semicolons** are used to show more than one pronunciation. The most common pronunciation usually comes first.
7. **Abbreviations** in small italic letters tell the part of speech. As examples: *n = noun, v = verb, adj. = adjective, adv. = adverb, pron. = pronoun, prep. = preposition,* etc. [i.e., charm *tverb*] *tverb = transitive verb.*
8. **Numbers** at the beginning of each definition are used to tell the number of definitions for each word.

Some definitions also include synonyms *<syn.>* (words that mean the same thing) and antonyms *<ant.>* (words that mean the opposite).

Helpful Hint for Learners

The first thing you need to know is that not all dictionaries list every word. Beginning dictionaries, found in elementary schools, usually carry a fundamental representation of the language—about six thousand of the most commonly used words. Dictionaries in middle-school classrooms and high-school classrooms provide between ten thousand and fifteen thousand words, and are adequate. A collegiate dictionary will carry most words—anywhere from sixty thousand to one hundred thousand words—but not even these list everything.

Dictionaries are essential reference tools for emerging, and even fluent, readers. Everyone benefits from using a hard copy, paperback, or online dictionary!

Additional Learning Activities

Within reason, English language learners should keep an appropriate dictionary handy whenever they are reading. The more "new" words you look up, the larger your usable vocabulary becomes.

Every month, *Reader's Digest* has a section titled "It Pays to Increase Your Word Power." We highly recommend it to anyone who wants to build an outstanding vocabulary!

Summary

To use a dictionary efficiently, alphabetizing is necessary to locate words. Then, start a dictionary search by using guide words. Next, look at the pronunciation key and accent marks to determine how to pronounce the word properly. Finally, read through the definitions to select from the multiple meanings provided.

CSML-030: MULTIPLE MEANINGS OF WORDS

Vocabulary Development Skills 2

Introduction

Clarify meanings of many familiar words by their multiple meanings. *Multinyms* are words whose meanings (and pronunciations) vary with context. The *denotation* of a word is the primary definition (*literal meaning*), and the *connotation* is the interpretation of the word with its emotional meaning.

Consider that a word is rarely just a word made up of specific letters; it usually has more than one meaning and may have significance beyond its definition. It frequently has overtones, and it means only what a person thinks it means!

As was discussed in "Dictionary Uses" (CSML-029), many of the publishing standards used in this unit are excerpted from the Collegiate Edition of *Merriam Webster's Deluxe Dictionary* published by *Reader's Digest*.

Prerequisites for Learning

Learning to use a dictionary is possible at almost every age and language skill level of "emergent" and above. Knowledge of alphabetic sequence is important, as are distinguishing and understanding letter and syllable sounds and familiarity with the different parts of speech (noun, verb, preposition, etc.). At the emergent level, using an elementary-level dictionary is recommended. For more advanced levels, use a hardback or paperback collegiate dictionary. Of course, online dictionaries are also great!

Why Do We Need to Know This?

Any exercises calling attention to similarities and differences in word meanings help strengthen vocabulary, comprehension, and the ability to communicate concise meanings. In a dictionary, abbreviations are used to identify synonyms (*syn.*) and antonyms (*ant.*). These usually appear after a word's last definition. You will note in these listings that the list of antonyms is generally the opposite of the list of synonyms.

Vocabulary Skills Development

- knowing multiple meanings of the same word
- understanding the definitions
- selecting the correct definition for the context
- being able to recognize that the different parts of speech (nouns and verbs, for example) may be spelled and sound the same but may have entirely different meanings)

Learning Activities

Practice multinyms by combining reading with practice dictionary exercises. When doing this, the goal is to recognize the proper in-context interpretation of a word by substituting differing dictionary meanings to decide which meaning is most correct to complete the meaning of the sentence. To refine this process, learners should practice how to deliberately infer meaning from what went before and, if necessary, reading ahead for clues to meaning. It is like being a detective.

Key elements in understanding how multiple meanings can occur within the English language are to recognize the four different forms of multinyms:

1. **Synonyms** (from the Latin root *synon*, meaning similar or same) are words meaning the same or nearly the same as the word used. Examples: help/assist, frigid/cold.

2. **Antonyms** (from anti-, meaning opposed to or opposite) are words opposite or nearly the opposite of another word. Examples: help/resist, frigid/boiling.

3. **Homonyms** (words that sound the same). Examples: their/their, whether/weather, fair/faire, course/coarse, aloud/allowed, whole/hole, piece/peace, hear/here, raise/rays, etc.

4. **Heteronyms** (words which are spelled the same but are pronounced differently). Examples: tear/tear, lead/lead, read/read, etc.

Helpful Hint for Learners

Any exercises calling attention to similarities and differences in word meanings help strengthen vocabulary and comprehension. Practice also helps build awareness of the importance of spelling in preparing accurate and understandable written communications.

Additional Learning Activities

Within reason, English language learners should keep a dictionary handy whenever they are reading anything. The more "new" words they look up, the larger their usable vocabulary becomes.

Summary

To use a dictionary efficiently, alphabetizing is necessary to locate words. Then, start a dictionary search by using guide words. Next, look at the pronunciation key and accent marks to determine how to pronounce the word properly. Finally, read through the definitions provided to select from the multiple meanings provided. Pay careful attention to the different uses of a word since the meaning and pronunciation of many words can depend on its context.

CSML-31: FIGURATIVE LANGUAGE AND IDIOMS

Vocabulary Development Skills 3

Introduction

As we read this mini lesson, you notice we are moving away from the linguistic nuts and bolts. We are entering a world where language takes on meaning and can be really enjoyable!

Authors use language to convey moods and create effects through the use of different forms. The enjoyment and appreciation of literature is enhanced by a variety of things.

Students recognize imagery, understand figurative language and allusions, see how language portrays tone and mood, notice the effect of word order and rhythm in prose and poetry, and discover the theme of a text or story matter. Evaluating and responding to literature is the primary goal of any language arts/reading program.

Language learners also benefit from assistance with the English language's quirky idioms, groups of words, or sayings such as "I'm all ears." English as Second Language learners have a more challenging time with idioms since they may not make any sense.

Idioms offer color and zest to all the conventions mentioned above. When students master idioms, their writing is more interesting, and they boost their reading comprehension. There are other language structures in this lesson that you will find interesting and enjoyable to teach and learn.

Prerequisites for Learning

We now move from the technical aspects in studying English to what is often referred to as "culturally-embedded" vocabulary. Much of this comes from stories and events many children learned at their mother's knees. *Aesop's Fables*, the stories of Hans Christian Andersen, *Grimm's Fairy Tales*, and other literature offer a look into the foundation of much of our unique language.

Why Do We Need to Know This?

A great deal of descriptive American English vocabulary has its roots within the American culture. There are two major aspects to this vocabulary. *Figurative language*, the larger of these groups, is made up of five components: metaphors, similes, personification, hyperbole (the *e* is pronounced as a separate hard vowel), and allusion. The second group is *idiom*, a style or dialect of language peculiar to a specific group, geographic area, or culture. Some experts believe that idiomatic language can be so intense that it becomes a language in its own right.

Figurative Language

Simile

A simile is an analogy in which two dissimilar things are shown as being alike (similar). One of the easiest ways to identify a simile is the use of words such *as like, as,* or *than.*

- The blue jay screamed like a noisy child.

Metaphor

A metaphor is an analogy comparing, but, unlike the simile, the words *like* and *as* are not used. A metaphor may be a particular word, phrase, or sentence suggesting a similarity between two things.

They are two peas in a pod, all the world is a stage, a marshmallow cloud, a river running down the middle of the street, etc.

Personification

Personification is a literary technique giving human actions or traits to animals or objects.

- "The Bible tells us ..." instead of "We read here, in the Bible ..." and is also commonly used to give voices and human emotions to animals in cartoons, theater, and children's literature.

Hyperbole

A hyperbole is an obvious exaggeration or overstatement using words like grand, horrid, unique, etc. They are generally used to create an image obviously larger than life.

- That baby weighs a ton!
- In her eyes, he stood every bit of twelve feet tall.

Allusion

An allusion is an indirect reference to a person, real or mythical, or to a place or thing, when describing another person, place, thing, or event.

- "She liked living in a Taj Mahal" describes the enjoyment of a woman living in a palatial home. ("A Taj Mahal" might be used to describe any such residence, and "*the* Taj Mahal" identifies the specific historic structure).

Idiomatic Language

Idioms

Idioms are components of a language particular to a people (culture) or to a district, community, or class. They make up a dialect of an overarching language and often display the syntactic, grammatical, or structural forms peculiar to a language. In literature, they are used as a display of the stereotypic speech associated with specific groups or geographic areas.

Some examples of this might be seen in the Georgian drawl ("Hi, there, y'all!") or a "Texican" mix of properly used purely Anglo and purely Hispanic words in the same sentence (such as "hot tamale). Over time, many of these words and phrases have been "adopted" into our basic language and are believed to have English roots.

Learning Activities

Figurative language and idioms are best learned by immersion, not by memorizing. The best, most effective, and most enjoyable way to fully understand figurative language and idioms is to read widely across multiple genres of the English literary world. Find out where and when the legends came from: Paul Bunyan, Johnny Appleseed, Tom Sawyer, Huckleberry Finn, and Shoeless Joe Jackson (both the man and the legend). Read *See Spot Run, Aesop's Fables*, Dr. Seuss stories, *Moby Dick*, and *The Rime of the Ancient Mariner*. Learn about the "villains" and "heroes" of the Old West, *The Wizard of OZ, The Adventures of Alice through the Looking Glass*, and *The Old Man and the Sea*.

Discuss what you are reading, both in and out of school, with your family and friends. As you continue reading, you will find yourself growing in an understanding of who you are, where you came from, and even what your personal future might hold for you.

Helpful Hints for Learners

The best way to handle these vocabulary components is to understand that they are simply interesting, colorful ways of describing or understanding comparisons, emotions, and other aspects that make our language as diverse and expressive as it is!

Additional Learning Activities

Take any printed text, newspaper, magazine, and even a product sales catalog and read three or four pages of text, marking each of the figures of speech as you go along. If you are doing this for academic purposes, identify each of these as:

- (A) allusion
- (H) hyperbole
- (I) idiom
- (M) metaphor
- (P) personification
- (S) simile

Note that these figures of speech are not in order of use or importance. They are just placed in alphabetical order.

Summary

The American-English language is incredible in its width, depth, and ability to convey precise information and meaning as well as a magnificent diversity in descriptive and inspirational literature. A good part of this comes from the ability to involve the reader emotionally in the text.

These five tools are part of the human side of the language, but many have become part of technical and business communication methods as well.

CSML-032: TECHNICAL LITERACY

Vocabulary Development Skills 4

Introduction

People in almost every occupation and profession have their own unique ways of expressing themselves clearly and precisely to other members of the group. Although dictionaries are the primary source for spelling, pronunciation, and meaning of words, technical language usually is not covered.

Prerequisites for Learning

While learning is possible at almost every age and language skill level of "emergent" and above, a language proficiency level of advanced is recommended.

Why Do We Need to Know This?

The ability to "talk the talk" is considered a hallmark of employability. A great deal of the unique words and phrases are learned "on the job."

Students need to be aware of their culture's demand that workers be able to communicate within their own specific discipline and with the general public.

Learning Activities

Select any professional-level book, handbook, or manual. Most of this publication specialty will contain an alphabetical index and a glossary of terms, a section of words, terms, and phrases that are not defined within a general-purpose book.

A reader should always approach *any* text with several questions. Among these are:

- Question 1: "Why am I going to read (or why am I reading) this material?" (motivation for learning)
- Question 2: "What do I already know about the subject?" (foundation for learning)
- Question 3: "Do I have enough background to understand what I am reading?" (prerequisite for learning)
- Question 4: "Why should I be able to expect that this material is appropriate for my goals?" (understanding resources)
- Question 5. "What do I expect to know about this subject when I am finished reading?" (predicting and questioning)

Instructional Activities

Despite the fact that these common sense mini lessons are focused on learning how to read more effectively and with better understanding, it may often sound like a lesson deals more with writing than with reading. This is because reading and writing are two sides of the same coin. People read what others have written, and they write for other people to read.

Everyone needs to know certain basic principles and forms of communication. This is true for functioning successfully in highly technical work environments or simply in everyday social situations.

For example, you have just found a coupon in the newspaper. It is for a really good discount for something you would really like to own. But when you look at it, you notice that there is no address or phone number for the store. You also notice that the coupon will not be good until next Wednesday. There may be several other branches of the store in town, but you don't know where to go—and you have to call to get the location and store hours.

How important do you think it is to be able to find everything you need to know within the written material to understand what you are reading?

When someone is reading, he or she brings a certain level of understanding to the task. Unfortunately, in technical writing, it is often understood that level of understanding is present. But this is rarely the case. Here are some examples:

- "Tighten the bolt to fifty pounds of torque."
- Everybody knows that you tighten a bolt by turning it in a clockwise direction and how to measure fifty pounds of torque, right? But be careful because this is a fairly small and delicate bolt with a left-hand thread that tightens counter-clockwise, and it will be stripped threadless if you try to tighten it to fifty foot-pounds instead of the more desirable fifty inch-pounds.

Look out for an author's shorthand in a recipe book:

- "Measure ½ t salt and add to the mix."
- Is that half a teaspoon or half a tablespoon? Do you add it to the mix by stirring, blending, folding, or using an electric mixer?

Then there's the note from your dad telling you not to forget to put the gas can in the car! Are you supposed to put the empty can into the trunk or are you supposed to pour the gas in the can into the gas tank? (We will assume he didn't mean to pour in into the back seat or under the hood onto a hot engine).

Many professional technical writers are painfully aware of how important this degree of completeness and accuracy can be—and how often inexperienced writers overlook it. Just for the fun of it, think of how many ways: "Would you please get the car out of the garage?" can be miscued—and how many problems a misunderstanding can cause. Here is a partial list:

- Do you know how to drive?
- Do you have the keys?

- Which car? (Assuming there is more than one car in the garage.)
- Is the garage door open?
- Is the door blocked by another car?

Suppose you have just found this note on the kitchen table. *Would you like to go out to dinner this evening?*

Now do the same exercise. How many details are missing? What are they?

As a reader, you have every right to expect the material you read to be clean, clear, properly structured, and with content and detail appropriate to whatever that material might be. If you need an interpretive guide to read a technical manual, a textbook, or a thing as simple as an invitation or a note, that material is incomplete. And this kind of "stuff" is around us every day, especially in advertising content.

Helpful Hints for Learners

Communicating in—and understanding of—many of the words and phrases can also be accomplished when they are viewed as:

- Abbreviations—words that are not words but are often used in the place of a word with a specific professional or organizational setting.
- Acronyms—words constructed using the first letter of every significant word within a title, name, or phrase.
- Compound words—words created by connecting them to form a single word specific to the applying profession.
- Words that are developed using affixes—infixes, prefixes, and suffixes.

Additional Learning Activities

Select any work that you are not familiar with and interview a working professional. Explain that you are studying how different professions have developed their own precise terms and definitions.

In construction, for example, the term "rebar" is used to identify reinforcing steel bars used in concrete-based construction. And in plumbing, a snake is a tool for clearing pipe blockages—not a potentially dangerous reptile.

Now identify the professional with whom you are speaking and the title of the profession.

The same practice of creating special words or phrases carries over into sports.

- Who or what is "cleanup" in the batting order?
- Who or what is a "hindsnatcher," and in what sport is it applied?
- What sport uses a key, and what does it mean?
- What is a "quarter horse," and in what sport or trade is the term used?

Pick up any age-appropriate publication (book, magazine, newspaper, or computer article) and read through several pages. While you are reading, make notes of any questions that come to mind. See how many of these questions are answered within the text.

Summary

When reading for understanding, using a dictionary is always appropriate—and often essential. But it should never be a requirement to understand a written message. In written communications, understanding is the responsibility of the writer *and* the reader.

CSML-033: SPELLING RULES

Reading and Writing Skills Development

Introduction

We have already reviewed many elements of word study, such as individual sounds, to gain clues to what an entire word might be and how to use context to find the meaning of a word.

But there is another important skill, accurate spelling, that also helps in understanding meaning. More important than that is how much spelling properly really counts. It might affect your ability to pass tests, makes your writing readable, and might influence whether you are hired or not.

Prerequisites for Learning

Learning to spell properly requires that the student and the teacher are capable of hearing and enunciating words read or spoken in common English. Spelling is a matter of being able to read (decode) and write (encode) a wide variety of words.

Why Do We Need to Know This?

As you read in the introduction, spelling well greatly affects your life. The ability to spell correctly is often used as a gauge of the intelligence and education of writers. It can also be the controlling factor in looking up words.

Learning Activities

There are many fundamental rules for proper spelling, many of which are based in the origin of the word. But there are ten high-utility (very useful) rules the student should be aware of when learning to spell.

1. In the English language, *q* is almost always followed by a *u*. Their combined sound is the same as *kw*, which is why *quick* often appears as *kwik* in advertising phrases and comical ducks often *kwak* instead of *quacking*.
2. Soft *g* (the *j* sound as in George) and soft *c* (the *s* sound as in *city*) are usually followed by either *i, y,* or *e*.
3. The letters -*dge* (as in ridge) are used after short vowels, and -*ge* (as in page) is used after long vowels. Both, however, are pronounced with the *j* sound of the soft *g*.
4. Usually, words end in *le*, not in *el*. Exceptions are something that will require memorizing. Examples are: tumb*le*, and humb*le* but not bush*el*.
5. After a short vowel, put a *t* in before *ch* (as used to *stretch*, but not used to *reach*.)
6. If a word sounds like *f*, but *f* is wrong, use *ph* to phone and *gh* to *cough*.
7. Words that identify an occupation or a profession usually end in *er* (teacher, plumber, lawyer) in *or* (as in doctor, professor), in -*ist* (as in economist), or in -*ician* (as in *physician* or *beautician*).
8. Add a prefix to a root word, and the root word remains the same. Examples are *misspell* and *mislaid*.

9. When adding a suffix to a word ending in *y* where the *y* is preceded by a consonant, change the *y* to an *i*. An example is *silly/sillier*.

10. To make a word ending in *y* a plural, change the *y* to *i* and add *es*. Examples are *baby/babies, city/cities*.

Students go through developmental spelling stages. The first of these is *prephonic*, starting to use letters to stand for sounds. Next comes *emerging phonic* where more letters are understood, but some may be omitted from words. This is especially true when dealing with silent letters.

Children begin working with the structure of the language next in the sequence and then begin using meaning, especially in root words.

"Inventive" and abbreviated (acronymic) spelling should transition to correct spelling before the third-grade skill level. Always provide correct models for students and provide corrections tied to a common practice or a rule whenever possible.

It is possible at any age and stage to improve spelling, but *third grade is considered a key skill level*. We tend to avoid nonsense words and use only correct spellings as models. Inventive spelling by children is a natural stage and should transition to correct models as early and quickly as possible. Model everything correctly!

Helpful Hint for Learners

Dictionaries are always excellent reference tools when looking for the correct spelling of a word.

If you cannot find a word using proper phonetic spelling, start applying rules that change the word's structure.

Common spelling errors occur when transitioning from singular to plural, from singular to possessive, and from the basic form to a contraction.

One example is *its*, which is the *plural or possessive form of it*, which is often misspelled as *it's*, which is the contraction *it is*. One way to avoid this is to remember the most common application for an apostrophe is to indicate a missing letter.

And here is rule number 11: *I before e except after c* … usually!

Additional Learning Activities

Every reading experience provides an opportunity to learn correct spelling. Generally, anything in print that is not in quotation marks will be spelled correctly.

Whenever you run into a new word, make a note of both the word and its meaning. And remember, when all else fails, reach for your Webster.

Summary

Proper spelling has a lot of rules. Some rules are dictated by structure, some are dictated by the origin of the word, and some simply are dictated by common practice. The most important thing is that you can either learn by rote (spelling words in isolation) or by context. It is the context-based method that proves the most useful in the real world.

Note to Coaches

Practice each type strategy in various written materials. Start with easy text and progress to more difficult (and challenging) reading materials. Cueing can provide extremely valuable skills if they are reviewed and practiced at each progressive learning level and across every level of content.

CSML-034: BASIC ENGLISH GRAMMAR

Skills Development

Introduction

As your student begins or reviews the study of oral and written English language you need to understand that words have special uses, some are names, and some describe. Every single word has a function: it does something.

This common sense mini lesson deals with two major elements of sentence structure: parts of speech and rules of capitalization.

Why Do We Need to Know This?

People often judge your intellectual and educational abilities by oral and written language. These include grammar (both speaking and writing), capitalization, and spelling (writing skills). The ability to express one's self clearly, to project skills and confidence in the four basic areas of communication: listening, speaking, reading, and writing play critical roles in work and social environments.

Instructional Activity

Parts of Speech

Words are divided into nine categories, according to their usage in the sentence. These nine parts of speech are:

1. **Nouns:** A noun is the name of something, a person, place, or thing. A *proper noun* names a particular person or object. A *common noun* names any one of a class or group of objects.

2. When you speak of *a student* (any individual within that group), you are using a *common noun*, but when you speak of a specific student, *John Jones*, you are using a *proper noun*.

3. **Pronouns:** Pronouns are words standing in the place of a word without specifically naming it. Typical pronouns are *I, you, he, she, it, we, you,* and *they.* An "antecedent" of a pronoun is the name of the person or object that takes the place of pronoun.

4. **Verbs:** Verbs are words used to denote action (action or "transitive" verb) or a state of being (be verb). Verbs are then defined by tense to indicate past, present, or future.

5. **Adjectives**: Adjectives are words that modify (describe or define) nouns or pronouns. Adjectives that indicate a limit to or describe a specific group of persons or objects are called descriptive adjectives. Proper adjectives, such as words like American or British, are always capitalized.

6. **Articles:** A specialized class of adjectives (referred to as definitive adjectives), articles such as *a, an, the, this,* and *that,* are signal words that the following word is a noun (or in some cases, a pronoun).

7. As an example of a sentence using each of the above word classes: if you are speaking about a car, and you use adjectives to specify "That (article) car (common noun) is (be verb) a (article) blue (descriptive adjective) Chevrolet (Proper noun.)

8. **Adverbs:** Adverbs are words used to explain or clarify the meaning of a verb, an adjective, or another adverb. Adverbs answer questions such as *who, where (place), when (time),* and

how (manner). Example: John (noun) quickly (adverb, modifying the verb) ran (action verb).

9. **Prepositions**: Prepositions, also known as connectives, are used to connect or show relationships between ideas. A preposition is a word used to connect a noun or pronoun with other words: *at, to, from, of, with, into, at, by, in, under, over,* etc.

10. **Conjunctions:** A subgroup of prepositions, conjunctions join words or groups of words: *unless, although, until, before, after, because, as, if,* etc.

11. **Interjections**: Words used to express sudden feeling: Oh!, Ah!, Hurray! Ouch! etc.

Rules of Capitalization

Here are eight rules to help you avoid most capitalization pitfalls!

- Begin the first word of every sentence with a capital letter. (Sorry, e-mailers and text messengers, but it really does make a difference to a lot of people.)
- Use capital letters for every proper noun and proper adjective. (*California, Californian.*)
- Capitalize the days of the week and months of the year. (*Monday, April*)
- Begin every direct quotation with a capital letter. (*"We hold these truths to be self-evident."*)
- Begin every personified noun (names, specific places, titles of specific activities) with a capital letter. (*Jerry Brown, California, Governor.*)
- Capitalize historical events, such as *the American Civil War.* (Notice that the definitive article *the* is not capitalized.)
- Capitalize the important words in the title of a book (or any other published text). Remember the first rule, but other articles are not capitalized. (*The Day the Earth Stood Still.*)
- Capitalize the sections of the United States, such as *Northwest,* unless you are referring to any portion of a smaller political

unit as a direction from point to point such as *central Kansas* or *Chicago is located northeast of St. Louis.*

Additional Learning Activities

Like every other skill, the English language demands constant practice and refinement. When you are writing something—anything—take the time to make sure your spelling is appropriate for your audience and you have paid attention to basic grammar rules. Under English law, there is always a final appeal to the Crown, but in English grammar, there is no appeal. You are judged by what you say and how you say it, by what you write and how you write it.

Summary

Proper English grammar has a lot of rules. They are the rules by which we judge the communicating ability of our fellow English speakers or writers. In all cases, these parts of speech are fairly straightforward. A noun is a noun is a noun (usually), and a verb is an action word—*transitive* (except when it isn't, then it is *intransitive*). Some rules are dictated by their purpose, and some simply are dictated by common practice. The most important thing is that you can either learn these rules by rote or by context.

CSML-035: COACH'S EVALUATION GUIDE

Author's Note

This brief handbook is intended for use by reading teachers or coaches merely as an introduction to Corrections and Interventions (CSML-036) and Informal Reading Inventory (IRI) (CSML-037). Correcting reading errors and difficulties is important for the new or reluctant, struggling reader (of any age).

Introduction

With high-stakes testing driving instruction, the pressure is really on to make sure kids know what they are decoding. Reading experts no longer call problems *errors*. The newer term is *miscues*. If we go back about a hundred years, reading errors were reading errors.

Emerging or underachieving readers are taught more quickly when we understand the miscues, or mistakes, that are being made. The following section, Corrections and Interventions, assists you with techniques and practices to remediate common reading errors and difficulties.

Miscue analysis allows the coach to observe and record the student's oral reading. Using an Informal Reading Inventory (IRI) and recording the types of errors enables you to decide which lessons you need to reteach and when to proceed. The reading mini lessons in this series help you accelerate the reading process. You may want to record one of these diagnostic sessions; if not, definitely take notes.

Listen for these most common types of miscues/errors:

- **Substitutions**—The student substitutes one word for another.
- **Insertions**—The student adds words not in the sentence.
- **Omissions**—The student leaves out letters, words, or phrases in either or both silent and oral reading.
- **Reversals**—The student makes reversals, as with the letters b and d or words such as was and saw. (*Check for dyslexia or other optical problem.*) (Note, reversals may be considered normal for beginning prereaders and emerging readers).
- **Repetitions**—The student rereads words and phrases.
- **Incorrect Phrasing**—Word "transpositions" such as "Fifth District Assembly" instead of "Fifth Assembly District."
- **Guesses Words**—The student attempts to guess the sound of unfamiliar words.

Properly identifying a student's Reading Level is important. Students become frustrated when they are trying to read materials that are too hard for their current skill levels. However, if a student shows an interest in a subject, it might be appropriate to go ahead with the material. Just provide more support and assistance—and allow more time for mastery. Usually it is better to teach at the independent or instructional level instead of the frustration level.

CSML-36: CORRECTIONS AND INTERVENTIONS

Word Studies: Miscues

Introduction

Reading levels are significant. Remember, students become frustrated when they are trying to read materials that are too advanced for their current skill levels. However, if a student shows an interest in a subject, it might be appropriate to go ahead with the material, just provide more support and assistance.

As an informal measure, ask the student to put down one finger on a page each time there is an unknown word; after five fingers, select another book. This is easy (and, no surprise here, it is called the five-finger technique). Professional educators have used this technique with hundreds of children of all ages because it works consistently and kids like to do it. There is nothing more frustrating than seeing a student struggling—and then giving up—because of stumbling over every word on a page.

Reading proficiency assessment, whether formal or informal, is usually defined in three levels. At the lowest of these, *the frustration level*, students may lack motivation and be frustrated by their lack of success. Patience, support, and encouragement are vital at this level.

As skills emerge, and reading confidence starts to appear, students progress into *the instructional level* where they focus, under supervision, on word recognition and comprehension skills. They start to exhibit a willingness to take risks and guess at words that seem familiar. At the frustration and instructional levels, miscues and errors are readily apparent. This instructional handbook deals primarily with these problems and provides some quick tips for intervention and correction.

The most advanced, *the independent level*, is reached when the student can function alone with little support. Minor errors and difficulties can be expected, but these are minimal. Continue reading instruction as the complexity of the material increases.

Instructional Activity

Why Do We Need to Know This?

Learning to read is not an overnight process. Even the best readers have problems from time to time, but at the beginning, it can be intimidating. Readers at the frustration level, especially young children, may be moved to tears by the results of their efforts to master what seems to be an impossible task.

One of the first things you need to know as a learning coach—and your students need to understand—is that becoming a skilled reader takes time and practice. Making mistakes is part of the learning process. Emerging readers, at any age, need to be encouraged as much as they need to be corrected. But in the end, watching a student become a self-motivated, independent reader and lifelong learner is a most rewarding process for everyone involved. The only way to never make a mistake is to never do anything, but that is the biggest mistake anyone can ever make!

Whether a reading coach or a reading student, you should begin by listening for these kinds of miscues (errors):

- **Substitutions**: If a student is substituting one word for another, work with the student to make flash cards of the challenging words. Then work on the beginning sounds or syllables that are difficult. Add problem words to the student's "sight words" sheets and use these words in sentences.
- **Insertions**: If a student adds words that are not in the sentence, do "read-alongs." Model pointing to each word (moving from left to right) as the student reads it, and encourage the student to do the same. For added emphasis, ask the student to lift a finger and bring it down for each word read, as it is being spoken.
- **Omissions**: Omissions are letters, words, or phrases that are left out of oral and silent reading. Usually, this can be a result of a tracking problem and if the problems persist after several attempts at corrective intervention, a visit to an optometrist might be recommended.

As an intervention, however, try using a paper guide, a ruler, or a bookmark under each line of print to help the eye follow the line from left to right. Other remedies might include building a larger sight-word vocabulary or using "read-alongs" and "choral reading," which is one-on-one reading out loud together.

Yet another helpful activity, "echo reading," is reading quietly, almost under the breath, while the student is reading along. In this case, the best beginning is to model the activity by having the student doing the almost quiet reading while you are reading aloud. Then, once the pattern is established, exchange the roles.

- **Reversals**: It is normal for younger emerging readers to make reversals, as with the letters *b* and *d* or shorter, one-syllable words such as *was* and *saw*. Sometimes, students just do not know the difference between left and right. If the problem continues after lightweight corrections, use the following remedial activities.
  - o Emphasize left *from* right, and then reading from left *to* right (normal reading for the English language). Then model paced reading with left-to-right hand

movement. Use flash cards to build sight vocabulary. You might also trace challenging words in cornmeal, salt, or shaving cream, onto sandpaper or other tactile material, especially when working with a tactile-kinesthetic learner.

o   Cover words with a card, or sentences with a piece of paper, which will allow the reader to uncover each word (or line) as the previous word (or line) is read. You might want to make a tachistoscope (a window marker card) by cutting a slot in a large index card or paper. The word, phrase, or sentence should show up in the window slit.

o   If you are working with worksheets or books that the student owns, another activity that can be used for reversal remediation is to color code the shape of the letters. This should also work well for *learning vowels and syl / la / bles*. You might also focus attention on proper reading order by marking the first letter of each word or marking the left margin of all the pages and reading practice papers to identify the left side.

o   And, finally, remember the "print-rich environment" and "word wall" learning environments? Marking the left side of everything makes it very hard to forget (or ignore).

•   **Repetitions**: If the student frequently rereads words or phrases, use material with more familiar words and phrases. Also, you might practice sounding out words (preferably syllable-by-syllable sounding out). Use this consistent way to recognize unknown words:

o   Look at the word (and sound it out).

o   See if any part of the word looks like an already known word.

o   How does it begin? / How does it end?

o   Read other words in the line; what do you think the word might be?

And, once again, do more work on building and practicing sight words.

- **Incorrect Phrasing:** This might be caused by insufficient sight vocabulary or simply by development of poor oral reading habits. This can be overcome by modeling proper phrasing.
  - o Learn or review proper phrasing by understanding the part punctuation takes place in the activity. Draw an analogy between punctuation marks and traffic signals: The period is a stop sign, the capital letter at the beginning of the sentence is a green light, etc.
  - o Reproduce reading passages / so they can / be divided into / two or three / (or even four or five) / phrases.
  - o Leave extra spaces (and even put in slash marks) to highlight the separations.
- **Guessing at Words:** There is no ongoing problem in an instructional-level reader guessing at a word from time to time, but when this happens during oral reading, it should be gently corrected immediately. Encourage the student to build and practice sounding-out skills and build additional sight words.
  - o Just for fun, see what you (or a student) can do with the missing words in the following passage: *
  - o Encourage the student to circle or _____ any guessed at words during silent _____. Then, using context clues, read the rest of the _____. (This, by the way, can easily be turned into a fun activity _____ will build skills for _____ in context.)
  - o As a last resort, use lower-level reading material, within the current instructional level, but do not be afraid to challenge a student. Teachers, especially in an overcrowded remedial-reading environment, may want to avoid challenging students for fear of their regressing back to the frustration level.
  - o Correct responses: *underline, reading, sentence, that, reading*

The preceding are among the most common miscues (errors). Others not dealt with here might be: word-by-word reading, monotone (lack of meaningful inflection), hesitations, losing place, or reading too slowly.

A Four-Step Contextual Approach to Mastering Strange/Unknown Words

Put a checkmark near the word or place a post-it note in the book margin and continue reading.

1. Next: After reading the sentence, passage, or paper, go back to the marked word.
2. If the meaning of the word is still unclear, try breaking it into its parts—prefix, root, suffix, etc.—and guess from what is recognizable.
3. Go to the dictionary and use pronunciation, definition, etc., as clues.
4. Make up a sight-word flash card with a definition and contextual use for future reference.

CSML-037: INFORMAL READING INVENTORY (IRI)

Word Studies: Miscues

Introduction

The Informal Reading Inventory helps determine both oral and silent reading skills. Usually, this consists of short passages at various difficulty levels. Use three tests, if possible: one for oral reading, one for silent reading, and a listening comprehension test. The resource guide at the bottom of this section has easy-to-use informal diagnostic titles that are perfect for at-home use.

Teaching skills relies on assessment: Use the diagnostic-prescriptive-evaluative cycle. Through standardized and other diagnostic tests, information regarding reading gaps is readily available. It is vital that you know your student's learning styles, interests, and needs. Gather this information through observation, conversations, and work products.

Of most importance, however, you need to motivate your student to want to read and to help him/her understand the importance of reading. The goal is to achieve championship reading skills and enhance the reader's self-esteem.

Your ultimate goal is to provide skills and results that last for a lifetime. Students can improve skills through independent practice, working alone, or working with a friend.

This mini lesson is prepared primarily for teachers, reading coaches, and parent-teachers. It is not intended to be considered a part of the instructional curricula provided within the common sense mini lesson series. Unfortunately, it is extremely difficult to deal with Informal Reading Inventory practices and evaluative methodology without infringing on copyright and other intellectual property rights.

EASY START READING INVENTORY GUIDE
SUGGESTED MISCUE IDENTIFICATION CODES
Applicable for Reading Skill Levels 1-8+ or gaps

PAGE ONE
STUDENT ID _____

DATE_____

It can be also be useful, when possible, to record the student's reading. Play this back with the reading material in front of the student. Have the student record his or her own errors using the following method.

Then, depending on the most frequently occurring errors, practice intervention strategies (review or re-teach to noted errors). Be sure the student's growth in Skills mastered, Skills to master, and the easiest Markup System for miscues, which includes the following:

1. "H"	Hesitates: Unsure of word or proper pronunciation. (See # 9)
2. "PE"	Wrong word pronunciation: Write the word.
3. "O"	Left out words or parts of words: Highlight or circle omissions.
4. "lll"	Reading word-by-word: Focus on sight word instruction.
5. "S"	Substitution(s): Write the substituted word above the error.
6. "I"	Insertions(s): Note the inserted word(s) above the sentence.
7. "~~"	Repetition(s): Wavy line shows repeated word or phrase.
8. "R"	Reversal(s): Write the word "reversed."
9. "P"	Pronunciation: Practice proper pronunciation, especially for vowels.
10. "?"	Guessing: Underline guessed (or unknown) word(s).
	As feasible, corrections and interventions should be applied as soon as possible. Verbal miscues can be handled in real time, while the inventory is being discussed with the student. Errors requiring review or re-teaching should be done as soon as lesson sessions are available but whenever possible, these activities should be handled before moving on to further reading materials.

Figure 37-1: Student Miscue Evaluation Coding

Reading Champs
EASY START READING INVENTORY
Applicable for Reading Skill Levels 1-8+ or gaps

PAGE ONE
STUDENT ID _____
DATE_____

Knows (+)	Needs (-)
1. Concepts about print	Conventions
2. Word Recognition _____ Letters / Alphabet	Letters
_____ Phonemic Awareness	Sounds Rhymes
_____ Consonants	Initial Medial Final Bossy 'R' Blends Digraphs 'Special' – y, w, s
_____ Vowels	Sounds Rules Digraphs Diphthongs Magic 'E' Vowel Teams
_____ Structural Analysis	Compound Words Contractions Syllables Roots Prefixes Suffixes

Figure 37-2: Easy-Start Reading Achievement (1)

Reading Champs
EASY START READING INVENTORY
Applicable for Reading Skill Levels 1-8+ or gaps

PAGE TWO
STUDENT ID _____
DATE_____

Knows (+)	Needs (-)
3. _____ **Oral Reading**	Pronunciation Reversals (Note Errors) Insertions Omissions Repeats Punctuation Phrasing Expression
4. _____ **Rate**	Automatic Fluent
5. _____ **Vocabulary**	Sight Words Synonyms Antonyms Homonyms
6. _____ **Spelling**	Syllables Word Families Basic Rules
7. _____ **Comprehension**	Main Idea Details Sequence Cause and Effect Compare and Contrast Other

Figure 37-3: Easy-Start Reading Achievement (2)

CSML-038: READING FOR UNDERSTANDING

Building Comprehension

Introduction

Having a purpose gives meaning to reading. Comprehension is the goal of reading, and therefore of reading instruction, at all levels. Comprehending and interpreting what is read is dependent upon *schema*, concepts acquired through past experiences. The word schema is singular; *schemata* is the plural. It simply means prior knowledge. When your student reads or you read, everything you read depends on prior knowledge. We all attach what we already know to new, unknown information.

Whether reading a novel or textual material, what is known before forms the basis for understanding. KWLW (see CSML-039) expands on the KWL chart originated by Donna Ogle in the 1970s.

K—what I already *know*
W—what I *want* to know
L—what I *learned*

The K and W are considered before reading, and the L follows after reading. When you ask what is already known or what the student wants to know, sometimes that is not a given—so just start reading. Usually, however, everyone has some sort of prior knowledge to attach the new learning or understanding to.

In order to comprehend a text well, it is critical to be able to understand the meanings of individual words, group words into units instead of reading one word at a time, and discern between main ideas and details. But the most important thing is having a purpose for reading, to be able to answer the question: *Why am I going to read (or why am I reading) this material?*

All readers bring meaning to words that serve as triggers to thought. Reconstructing experiences helps words take on meaning. Always take the time to determine background knowledge and fill in any gaps. In this handbook, we deal with the process of understanding and interpreting meaning and developing the tools to encourage a more in-depth style of reading.

Instructional Activity

Why Do We Need to Know This?

As we just stated, in order to comprehend a text well, the ability to understand the meanings of individual words, being able to group words into units instead of reading word-by-word, and being able to discern between main ideas and details, are all critical. But the most important thing is having a purpose to read, to be able to answer the question, "Why am I going to read (or why am I reading) this material?"

Understanding and Interpreting Meaning

Each of the following processes and skills is involved in comprehending reading material. The student masters the following mini lessons before going on to the next step:

- understanding the literal meaning of words, sentences, and paragraphs
- identifying the main ideas and finding important details
- following instructions

- seeing relationships and making comparisons
- predicting outcomes and solutions
- understanding the meaning of figurative language
- drawing conclusions and making generalizations
- seeing cause and effect

Armed with these abilities, the reader is prepared to answer the five key questions that motivate a person to read and promote the search for understanding the material to be read:

- *Why am I going to read (or why am I reading) this material?*
  Reading for a purpose requires that the reader understands why he or she is reading a particular text. If the student cannot answer this question, he or she may be reading *War and Peace* to learn about life on the Mississippi in the 1800s instead of enjoying *The Adventures of Huckleberry Finn.*

- *What do I already know about the subject?*
  Not a whole lot—except that it takes place along the southern part of the Mississippi River. I also know it is about a young boy and some of his friends, and there is a slave named Jim. The author was a guy by the name of Mark Twain who used to be a riverboat captain on the Mississippi.

- *What do I want to know (or learn) about this subject?*
  Maybe a little bit about what life was like back then—and why everybody thinks this book is so important.

  On the other hand, you may be interested in studying the techniques Twain uses to create the verbal scenarios and how colloquial dialect, figurative language, and idioms of the time draw the reader seamlessly from event to event and scene to scene.

- *What do I expect to find in this book about the subject?*
  Because the writer was a riverboat captain, he probably knew a lot about what it was like to live in the South, and maybe he even knew what kinds of trouble a kid could get into if he ran away from home.

After you have finished reading a little bit of the book, you are ready for some additional questions.

- *So far, what new information have I learned from reading this material?*
- *Is what I have read consistent with what I expected from reading this book?*
- *Am I gathering enough information, or am I enjoying this story enough, to continue reading?*

Related Mini Lessons and Additional Readings on This Topic

- CSML-031: Figurative Language and Idioms
- CSML-039: The KWLW Reading Strategy

The KWLW "Wall" Chart

K	W	L	W
Before Reading What do I already know?	Before Reading What do I want to know?	After Reading What have I Learned?	After Reading What would I like to learn next?

Figure 39-1: KWLW Wall Chart Template

CSML-040: STRUCTURAL FEATURES OF TEXTS

Organizational Patterns for Nonfiction Texts

Introduction

Informational text is also called expository text or infotext. This category of print media includes online articles, newspapers, textbooks, magazine articles, and other nonfiction materials.

Rachel Billmeyer and Mary Lee Barton of the McREL Educational Laboratory reviewed research on textbook organizational patterns and provided us with this summary of their findings:

1. *Generalized* text organizes by general statements usually followed by examples.
2. *Chronological* sequence organizes information based on a sequence through time.
3. *Episodic* text organizes by specific or key events, generally by sequence.
4. *Comparison and contrast* organizes information by identifying similarities and differences.
5. *Concept/definition* presents characteristics and examples.

6. *Descriptive* text organizes facts and objects by descriptions, usually beginning with the most comprehensive characteristics and progressing to the more definitive.
7. *Cause and effect* organizes through a sequential causal sequence.

Once the reader is familiar with the author's unique organizational pattern, it becomes easier to skim and scan for information and read with a specific purpose. Purpose for reading is closely connected to the reading response. Researcher Mary Tarasoff said, "Purpose creates the criteria for what information is relevant and irrelevant."

According to subsequent research, this statement provides the rationale for carefully forming or reading specific questions to be answered prior to reading texts to determine what answers might apply. The question forms a filter to focus more quickly and closely on only relevant information.

Prerequisites to Learning

We have completed most Reading Champs foundation work and understand structures that make reading more productive and enjoyable. At this level, learners should possess an adequate command of the English language and most (if not all) skills covered through CSML-034.

Instructional Activity

Why Do We Need to Know This

We "read for understanding."

- *Literal* level skills include following directions, recalling facts and dates, recognizing main ideas, and restating patterns and time lines (order and sequence of events).
- *Detail* questions are literal only if the reader can recall the answer without drawing on past experience or inferring from information presented in the text.

Understanding how the various categories of reading materials are structured enables us to move rapidly through large volumes of text in reasonable periods of time. For example, a properly organized news story should present the answers to the critical five questions (who, what, where, when, and why) within the first two paragraphs. A summary of the important facts occurs within the following two paragraphs. At this point, the reader can determine whether the information in the article is relevant to his or her interests.

Instructional Fundamentals

Knowing text features significantly affects comprehension. The best place to start is with a few success tips.

1. Be aware of a book's unique features, including layout, bold print, italics, bulleted lists and other materials, photos, graphs, charts, illustrations, and index aids.

2. Author Tony Buzan suggested that knowing how paragraphs (texts) are organized helps increase speed and comprehension. He described texts as *explanatory, linking,* or *descriptive.* In explanatory, which is the most common, look for the topic sentence or main idea near the beginning of the text, with details in the middle, and the conclusion near the end. This is the most common.

3. Sometimes an author writes with a different pattern. See if it is consistent. The main idea may be in the middle, or details may lead the reader to the most important idea at the end of each paragraph. Once in a while, an author writes the main idea in the middle—with details building to that main idea and details following. Finally, once in a while, the author is unclear, and the main ideas are anywhere in the paragraph. This calls for very close reading.

4. Peter Kump tells us there are five levels of information to look for in expository text:
   o the main idea (referred to in an essay as the thesis statement)

> o   the main point of each section or chapter (referred to in an essay as "arguments")
> o   the main point of each section in a chapter in a book or subsection in shorter works
> o   the main point of each paragraph
> o   the details within each paragraph

Instructional Practice

Model structural features of text and study skills for that particular text. The goals are to identify or review how to locate information using a book's structure and organizational pattern, select and evaluate information based on the purpose of the reading, and develop flexibility in rate techniques (dependent on purpose).

Before practicing the Book Walk (see CSML-041) regarding text features, there are a few other things you need to know. Speed-reader Howard Berg shares that a sentence's verbs and nouns offer the most important information. He also cautions to watch for negation words—such as *no, not,* or *can't* that may reverse meaning of a sentence.

Signpost and signal words add to or clarify meaning and tell the reader to shift gears. Common signal words are *before, then, next, moreover,* and *however.* The best authors use words that connect ideas and suggest transitions.

In almost every case, negations, signposts, and signals are going to be adjectives, adverbs, or prepositions. These modifiers include:

Qualifying words: *however, moreover, nonetheless, nevertheless,* etc. These are found at the beginning of a modifying phrase or sentence. *Nevertheless, this should not be viewed as a hard-and-fast rule.*

1. **Enumerative words**: *first, next, last, finally,* etc. Ordered lists, like this section of the text, are also in this category. *First, the reader wants to determine the actual meaning established by the word.*

2. **Contrast words**: *yet, otherwise, although, despite, in spite of, not,* etc. *Although this is generally true, it should not be viewed as a hard-and-fast rule.*

3. **Go-ahead words**: *such as, more than, that, moreover, likewise,* etc.

4. **Time signal words**: *before, since, earlier, later, to begin with, after, next, last, finally,* etc. To begin with, the reader must understand that these words and categories are really fairly arbitrary and are only definable in context. The word *context* is a composite word made up of the prefix *con* meaning "with or within" connected to the noun *text*.

5. **Connective words**: *if, so, therefore, however, even though,* etc.

Summary

When teaching structural features of text, whether a single page or a book, search for relevant elements because each work is unique. No two are exactly alike. Undoubtedly, some are going to be easier to read and understand than others, due to layout, sentence structure, concept development, or pattern of organization.

It is not uncommon for authors to combine patterns, particularly in longer passages. And when books are written by more than one author, there may be even more inconsistencies.

CSML-041: PREVIEW AND REVIEW OF TEXT

Reading Comprehension

Introduction

Preview and review of a text, includes using advance strategies such as KWLW, graphic organizers such as Venn diagrams or webs, and building background knowledge in the absence of schema or past experiences.

Previewing texts includes the processes of questioning, predicting, identifying concepts, brainstorming, and determining the purpose for reading.

The first step is to get to know the textbook. Let's start with an *Easy-Start Book Walk*. Find answers to twelve basic questions:

1. What is the title of the text, and when was it published?
2. Why does it matter when the text was written?
3. What do you already know about the author?
4. How do this book's unique features help you study?
5. Find the glossary, index, and appendices and explain the importance and techniques for using each of these.
6. What other aids are included in the text?
7. Are there questions at the beginning and/or end of each chapter?

8. Is there an introductory statement beginning each chapter?
9. Are summaries and conclusions provided at the end of each chapter?
10. Do you notice division and section headings?
11. Is vocabulary italicized, in bold print, or otherwise structured in the text?
12. What else do you notice that might help a student study the book?

To achieve the best results, the reader spends as much as 60 percent of the time previewing and defining the material (including taking notes and integrating material into a KWLW or graphic organizer), 30 percent of the time reading, and 10 percent of the time reviewing.

In many respects, this is very much like building a house or other structure; 60 percent goes into planning, identifying, and obtaining needed materials and the sequence in which they are to be used.

Instructional Activity

Why Do We Need to Know This?

It is a widely accepted fact that familiarity with a text improves both reading rate and comprehension. Knowledge of a writer's style and literary structure can further enhance the reader's enjoyment, thus achieving a unique bond between writer, text, and reader.

Previewing a text and becoming familiar with all its conventions is the path to achieving the goal of reading for comprehension, reading for enjoyment or, ideally, both.

Learning Activities

In the introduction to this mini lesson, we addressed twelve questions. Now let's provide some of the answers.

Examine the Textbook

1. *What is the title of the text and when was it published?* The title of a book, or the heading of any text, provides a clue to its subject. If a reader is looking for reading material dealing with American

history during the Revolutionary War period, he or she is not likely to find it in Jules Verne's *20,000 Leagues Under the Sea*.

2. *Why does it matter when the text was written?* A book on the American presidents published in 1958 will have no reference to President Kennedy, the first landing on the moon, or the era defined by the Viet Nam War.

3. *What do you already know about the author?* Knowledge about an author includes his or her writing style, authority in the subject area, political orientation, age, and more.

4. *How do this book's unique features help you study?* Readability of typeset, printed pages depends on a number of factors. First, text greater than seven inches should be laid out in a two-column format because eyes track best on columns of four inches or less. Type family, face, and size are also important—as is the contrast between the type and color of the paper. (Obviously we are not talking about reading online or using a Kindle, Nook, or other electronic devices).

5. *Find the glossary, index, and appendices and explain the importance and techniques for using each of these.* Each of these tools is intended to help guide the reader to a better understanding of the book's content. This is especially true in textbooks where the extensive amount of information requires tools to assist the reader.

6. *Is vocabulary italicized or in bold print or otherwise structured within the text? What other aids are included in the text? Bold-faced type* highlights the beginning of a subsection within a chapter or section. *Italic type* offsets longer quotations within a body of text. Superscripts and subscripts identify footnotes, endnotes, or references to appendices or tables. Headings might also be set off from the surrounding text with color or highlighting.

7. *Are there questions at the beginning and/or end of each chapter? Is there an introductory statement beginning each chapter? Are summaries and conclusions provided at the end of each chapter?* These are look-see questions asked to see how much learning/lesson plan thought has gone into developing the overall format of the text. It is not a matter of whether they

are there. It is more a matter of how well the text is organized. *Do you notice division and section headings?* Chapter, division, subdivision, and section headings should be formatted to stand out from the text body, usually in a different type family or font and clearly defined and consistent. Without this feature, separating information into easy-to-follow chunks is more difficult.

8. *What else do you notice that might help a student study the book?* Language and other content considerations should be appropriate to the age and learning level of the reader.

Take an Easy-Start Book Walk

Don't ask why—just do it! The answer becomes obvious as you go along.

- Read the front and the back of the book. They say you can't judge a book by its cover, but quite often, this is exactly what happens.
- Read the foreword and the introduction.
- Read the table of contents (the author's outline key to the organization of the book).
- Look at any charts, diagrams, pictures, glossary, index, etc.
- Notice any special features. Skim the book for format.
- Use an outline or web to build a concept map of the chapters.
- Look at the first and last chapters that introduce and summarize content.
- Look at the first and last paragraphs in the chapter that introduce and summarize subsets within the content.
- Identify the author's writing pattern.
- When "Book Walking" a text chapter, skim the entire chapter before reading it.
- Ask questions and make predictions about what information the book or chapter will provide.

Practice Activities

Tell the student to open the text to a particular chapter (your choice, not the student's). Allow sufficient time to preview the title, develop a purpose for reading, and grasp at least two main ideas from skimming in order to write a brief outline.

Practice *Mrs. Words'* (Rita's) *PWR* prereading strategy.

- The P stands for *predict*: Guess what the paragraph, page, or chapter is about.
- The W means *write* down the guess.
- The R stands for *reading*: Find out if the prediction is correct.

For the reading, use the Reading Champs *RCRC* strategy. *Read it! Cover it! Recite it! Check it!*

Finally, put it all together to do a *PWRCRC* exercise for pre, during, and post reading. Predict, write, read, cover, recite/retell, and check. This activity simplifies the reading preview and review process for both the student and teacher.

Related Mini Lessons and Additional Readings on This Topic

- CSML-039: The KWLW and KWLWW Reading Strategies
- CSML-042: Predicting and Questioning
- CSML-043: Selecting Main Ideas
- CSML-047: Question-Answer Relationships (QARs)

CSML-042: PREDICTING AND QUESTIONING

Reading Comprehension

Introduction

A reading champion becomes personally involved with the material before actually beginning reading. Making predictions and asking questions are keys to both reading rate and comprehension. The goal is to get an idea of the whole work, develop an interest in the topic, and determine prior knowledge about the subject. Instructors model how to predict what will happen next by considering background events, characters involved, and the situation.

Questions offer a road map of what to look for. Good readers continually ask questions and make predictions based on what is already known or what has already been read. They then read to find out if they are correct. Questions stimulate thinking because they force the reader to make use of prior knowledge and read between the lines; what is *not* said can often be as important as what is stated.

Why Do We Need to Know This?

The goal of predicting and questioning is to get an overview of the reading, develop an interest in the topic, and determine prior knowledge about the subject. A reading champion becomes personally involved with the material before actually beginning reading. Making predictions and asking questions are keys to both reading rate and comprehension.

Instructional Activity

Before reading, have the student do this basic *Easy-Start Book Quick Walk* exercise.

1. Think about the title. Why did the author choose this title? Does the title give clues to the content of the work?
2. Based on the title or the author, can you predict the content of the work?
3. Look for clues to the content, including setting, situation, and characters. Does there appear to be a relationship between these initial clues and the title?
4. Describe past experiences. How will the reader's experience with the subject and/or the author influence reading and feelings about the text?
5. Predict the theme (man versus nature, etc.).
6. Predict the possible outcome of the selection.

Instructional Practice

The ability to ask good questions focuses on these six basic comprehension skills, five of which are discussed in more depth in following mini lessons.
Recognizing main ideas (Refer to CSML-043.)

1. Organizing ideas (Refer to CSML-044.)
2. Seeing the sequence of ideas (See CSML-045.)
3. Noting details (Refer to CSML-046.)
4. Predicting and anticipating what will happen (Refer to CSML-047.)
5. Following directions

Here are some questions a reader might ask:

- What is the author's viewpoint (which may or may not the same as a main character's point of view)?
- What is the main idea (thesis, main plot, point of conflict, etc.)?
- What might be a good title (or another good title) for this selection?
- What facts does the author provide?
- Where/when did this event happen (is it real or fictional)?
- What happened first? Next?
- What does the reader think will happen next?
- What do you think will be the result or outcome?

Instructional Note

Reciprocal Reading is a great teaching practice. Following any reading chunk (sentence, paragraph, page, or chapter) ask the student questions about the reading before switching roles. The book remains closed during the responses. It is a simple, but powerful, method to model asking and answering questions. This is also an excellent method for studying a subject and reviewing for a test or other assessment.

CSML-043: SELECTING MAIN IDEAS

Reading Comprehension

Introduction

When reading text for understanding, it is necessary to locate essential ideas (themes). A paragraph is a set of consecutive sentences based on the same subject. The main idea or central thought of a paragraph is found anywhere in the text, including at the beginning, in the middle, or at the beginning and restated at the end; in some cases, it is not stated at all. The latter is most common in tales and fables where the main idea is often found in the unstated moral of the story.

Separating important ideas from their details (either explanatory or supporting) is essential to comprehension. Most paragraphs are built around a central theme, and while many ideas are stated plainly, others must be inferred. Struggling readers may concentrate on one or more of the details and remain unaware of the paragraph's broader meaning. What is this paragraph really about? What is the author saying?

Why Do We Need to Know This?

One of the important goals of reading is to extract deeper meanings from the surface details of the text, seeking cause-and-effect relationships, making generalizations, and drawing conclusions based on information provided. This is especially important when reading or writing in an academic environment.

Instructional Activities

A simple way to practice selecting the main idea is to provide a passage together with a choice of possible themes. The first objective is to make sure the student recognizes the topic of the passage, starting with a single paragraph. If that is too advanced, go sentence by sentence. Once the student is able to select key ideas in a single paragraph, he or she is ready to identify key ideas within a group of paragraphs surrounding a single thought. Therefore, begin work with the main ideas in a paragraph and finally a whole article or book.

How often have you read something and then walked away, shaking your head and saying, "Huh?" This is not uncommon, but within it is a technique for improving writing and making reading more understandable. More advanced skill level students can read the paragraph below and follow directions in the exercises to help read for understanding.

Many people think that something is written the same way it is spoken, but it is easy for this kind of writing to be misunderstood. Although we tend to rely on visual gestures and vocal inflection to convey our meanings, we just write it down and expect everybody to understand. This may get us by in e-mails, but when conveying important information, it can be inadequate.

One of the marks of good writing that goes hand in hand with reading for understanding is that the document should have a comfortable flow. It should follow a logical progression from one concept to another, sentence by sentence and paragraph by paragraph. It should take the reader from "This is where I am right now" to "This is where I expected to be when I started reading." Writing is as much a mechanical art as it an art form.*

Instructional Practice

As appropriate to student skill levels:

1. *Read the preceding passage: Explain the main idea in your own words. Assuming it is the introduction to a longer paper, would you (the student) say this is easily understood? Why or why not? Explain your thinking.
2. Using readings from another source—online article, textbook, or magazine—underline the main ideas in several paragraphs.
3. Write a paragraph using three or four sentences to state the main idea.
4. Use supporting details to help clarify the main points.
5. Match the main idea with the introductory and summary paragraphs of a chapter.
6. From a list of sentences, select the one that most clearly expresses the main idea.
7. Select the best of several possible titles that matches the main idea.
8. Find the single most important sentence or paragraph of a short selection.
9. State the difference between a main idea and a detail.

Explain why reading and writing both use main ideas and details. Why is it important that a reader clearly understand main ideas? Why should a writer clearly develop main ideas?

CSML-044: ORGANIZING AND SEQUENCING IDEAS

Reading Comprehension

Introduction

A fundamental comprehension skill, it is important that readers recognize and recall the sequence or order in which ideas are written. A sequential pattern can be developed as *chronological, spatial,* or *expository.* Look carefully since authors frequently use combinations of these patterns.

- *Chronological sequence* simply means that events are organized from beginning to end, from the oldest event to the most recent. One variation within this category is the flashback, where the writing begins with a picture of the outcome, and then goes back to tell the story from the beginning. Can you think of a recent movie that is based around flashbacks?
- A *spatial sequence* might be centered on a specific place and/ or time, but it is told from viewpoints in the same time frame. Another term often used for this sequencing is, "Where Were You When," which refers to events happening at the same time in different physical locations.

- *Expository sequence* is not defined by time or space but rather by facts or ideas. This is generally seen as cause and effect. If this happens, then this happens, as a result.

Why Do We Need to Know This?

To make sense of text, the student identifies logical sequence. It gives the work a means of being read much the same as a road map on a planned trip. Just as a GPS tells the desired route to follow, sequence offers the reader a step-by–step, logical way to understand the parts of the selection.

Imagine reading a history without a timeline.

Instructional Activity

Instructional Practice

- **The Chronological Sequence**

  As explained earlier, chronological sequence simply means that ideas are organized from beginning to end, from the oldest to the most recent. One variation within this category is the flashback, where the story begins with a picture of the outcome, and then goes back to tell the story from the beginning.

  To identify a work written in chronological order, skim through the table of contents, or through a given section, noting the bold headings. If the headings are organized along a timeline, take notes or outline the sequence. To assist recall, build a flow chart, timeline, indented outline, or similar graphic organizer.

  Read passages from a [good] cookbook and notice how the ingredients are usually listed in the order used, as are the recommended steps and detailed procedures. Likewise, a repair handbook is usually written so all sub-assemblies are built first, and then they and the remaining parts are assembled in a specific order to create the final product.

- **The Spatial Sequence**

  Spatial, the second sequence, is a descriptive ordering of area-to-area or region-to-region relations between events occurring within the same time period. A spatial organization allows a comparison of viewpoints. It also offers a stable pattern such as a map, a floor plan, or sketch of a route from one place to another.

  How a reader interprets the events is changed by the nature of time and space.

  Another term sometimes used to define this sequencing is "Where Were You When," which refers to events happening at the same time in different physical locations.

- **The Expository Sequence**

  Expository sequence is defined neither by time nor space but rather by the relationship connecting facts or ideas. The root word for *expository*—expose—is the defining factor, using an event to expose either its causes or its effects. Some recent examples of this kind of writing are seen in television series such as the CSI Trilogy of shows, the writings of Agatha Christie, Sir Arthur Conan Doyle's Sherlock Holmes mysteries, the bestselling Harry Potter series, or *The Hunger Games*.

  Writing is expository when it is organized by cause to effect, questions to answer, general statement to details or important factors (deductive reasoning), or details to the general statement (inductive reasoning). The most typical expository passage is deductive, so when practicing, look for a generalization and then for the causes.

  Think of the expository sequence as asking, "What happened?" "Why did it happen?" or "What did it cause?" One of the more interesting branches of the science fiction genre deals almost entirely with the question "What would (might) have happened if?"

Practice outlining, using a line or bar graph, Venn diagram, T-chart or other organizer to make comparisons and show relationships.

More Practice

- Tell what happened in chronological order. Organize simple sentences and paragraphs in correct order. Find answers to five Ws—who, what, where, when, why, and the H—how.
- Read the main ideas in a chapter to get a sequential overview of the material. Enumerate the steps of a process or a chain of historical events.
- Notice the words used that suggest the introduction of another step, such as *then, next, second, another, subsequently,* or *finally.*
- Note and graph the steps, in the proper order, for constructing something.
- List the chain of events leading to an outcome.

Applying What You Are Learning

To help a student fully understand the importance of sequencing, you might work with him or her in building a small, inexpensive model airplane, car, or similar three-dimensional item. Notice how each subassembly is built first, is joined with other subassemblies, and then is joined with the detail or trim parts to become the final product.

When is painting recommended?

- Are there any details or specifications included in the kit?
- Why is it important to follow the sequence of the assembly instructions?

CSML-045: FINDING AND CLARIFYING IMPORTANT DETAILS

Reading Comprehension

Introduction

More complex than sentence reading, paragraphs have a central thought and have more details that can confuse a reader. Good readers sort out details from main ideas and understand the relationships among sentences.

Instructional Activity

Why Do We Need to Know This?

Knowledge of sentence structure and punctuation helps the reader analyze sentences and paragraphs. Each paragraph contains a core thought (main topic) and details that are subordinate to the core thought. The reader's job is to separate the lesser information from the main idea and decide which details are most important to fully understand the main idea.

Most text is broken down into a central theme (referred to as the *thesis* of essays or other academic writings) and supporting details. If you were to look at the preceding paragraph with a very simplistic outline, it might look like this.

Purpose of this paragraph	To respond to the headlined question.
Paragraph (Main Topic) Lead sentence.	Knowledge of sentence structure and punctuation helps the reader analyze sentences and paragraphs.
Each sentence applies to the subject and provides additional or clarifying information.	Each paragraph contains a core thought (main topic) and details which are subordinate to the core thought.
This sentence provides the answer to the question, "Why do we need to know this?"	The reader's job is to separate the lesser information from the main idea and decide which details are most important to fully understand the main idea.

Figure 45-1: Thematic Text Analysis

In the table above, it is apparent that the preceding paragraph was written in an inverted structure.

The reader's job is to separate the lesser information from the main idea and decide which details are most important to fully understand the main idea. Each paragraph contains a core thought (main topic) and details that are subordinate to the core thought. Knowledge of sentence structure and punctuation helps the reader analyze sentences and paragraphs.

Each paragraph also contains a main idea and details that explain the main topic and clarify its overall meaning. As stated earlier, some paragraphs have *signal words* that alert the reader to what is coming next. Knowing the basic function of the paragraph also helps determine main ideas and supporting details.

First, the *introductory paragraph* introduces a subject. The next type of paragraph is called a *descriptive paragraph* because it further describes the idea that has already been expressed. Bridging the gap from one idea to another, the *transitional paragraph* uses words such as *however* or *but*. Finally, the *summary paragraph* restates or reinforces the main idea.

Within each type of paragraph, details (in the form of sentences) support the main idea. Determine which details, such as facts, names, or dates, are important to remember. Details support generalizations through evidence as supporting illustrations.

Applying This Knowledge—Making It Work

1. Find answers to specific questions.
2. Note relative importance of details through signal words/phrases such as *above all, most important, that having been said,* etc.
3. Note the importance of details by use of italics, pictures, and other graphic aids.
4. Notice how the author indicates the importance of details, such as spending more time on a set of detailed literal information.
5. Match a series of main ideas with a list of details.
6. Categorize the types of details.
7. Review functions of paragraphs by identifying each type.
8. Notice how grammar indicates upcoming details.

Summary

The process of finding details is at the *literal level* of comprehension. The student recalls details provided by the author. Details are important building blocks for forming concepts and relate to the main ideas they support and clarify.

CSML-046: SUMMARIZING

Drawing Conclusions—Making Inferences

Introduction

The skills of summarizing, drawing conclusions, and making inferences are woven closely together. Each is an important component skill in the practice of reading for understanding.

1. *Summarizing* requires identifying main ideas, noting the most important details, omitting irrelevant facts, and putting the information together in a sensible order. It also allows the reader to break down large blocks of text into a few words.
2. *Drawing conclusions* requires that the reader determines significant points and topic sentences, identifies the primary supporting structure (most relevant reasons and illustrations), and recognizes transitions.
3. *Making inferences* is an essential interpretive skill closely related to generalizing. When inferring, the reader draws a conclusion and simultaneously predicts an outcome.

Why Do We Need to Know This?

Summarizing, drawing conclusions, and making inferences are closely related. Mastering these comprehension skills enables students to compress an entire chapter into manageable, understandable building blocks.

Instructional Activity

Instructional Content

The best way to start this lesson is by looking at the root dictionary definitions of the three terms in the title of this handbook—*summary, conclude,* and *infer.*

- **Summary** (noun)—succinctly covering the main points of a body of text.

  The ability to summarize helps a student become a better reader by making the best use of main ideas, facts, and details in a paragraph. This means knowing how to locate important facts, separate major and minor details, and understand the sequence. The ability to use the QAR (Question, Answer, Respond) strategy, described in detail in CSML-047, is a bonus.

- **Conclude** (intransitive verb)—to bring to an end, especially in a particular way or with a particular action. Conclusions are based on cause, effect, and consequence.

  Effectively drawing conclusions is necessary for determining main points and topic sentences, identifying the primary supporting structure (the most important reasons and illustrations), and recognizing transitions.

  Ask, "What will happen as a result of the events or actions?" Make sure there is enough evidence or supporting information to draw a conclusion. Then base it on sufficient patterns of actions, events, or thoughts— logically putting the facts and details together.

- **Infer** (transitive verb) — to derive as a normal outcome from facts or premises.

Making an inference crosses content areas.

As pointed out in the introduction, making inferences is an important interpretive skill closely related to generalizing. When inferring, the reader draws a conclusion while predicting an outcome. When only partial information is given in a text, the reader must place the ideas in time and assess the mood or tone (the general effect or atmosphere).

Instructional Practice

Inferences

The instructor models the process of making an inference. The student identifies or restates the process.

Inferences can be made about location, time, action, category, cause and effect, or problems and solutions. Find examples of each.

- *Location:* "Once the dike had broken, all the surrounding fields were flooded with more than four feet of water." *Inference:* the territory around the river was normally under the level of the river.
- *Time:* "Although it was not visible in the dark, people could hear the train approaching from miles away." *Inference:* The event was taking place at night.
- *Action:* The giant, leather-winged reptile soared effortlessly over the steaming green valley. *Inference:* The reptile is likely a pterodactyl.
- *Category:* The street was lined with identical houses standing behind hedges and manicured lawns. *Inference:* The location is a suburban residential neighborhood.
- *Cause and effect:* The next morning, peaches and apples littered the orchards for miles. *Inference:* There had been a serious storm during the night.

- *Problems and solutions:* Week after week, trash piled up along the side of the road. *Inference:* Nobody was collecting and disposing of trash discarded by passing vehicles.

Inferences can also be made from asking six questions: *who, what, where, when, why,* and *how.* Locate examples of each:

- Routinely anticipate what is coming next in the text.
- Read a text and list word clues that helped support the inference.

Independent Practice

Summarizing and Drawing Conclusions

- choose the sentence that best summarizes the content of a paragraph
- select the best statement that summarizes a longer paragraph
- restate the author's main idea in one sentence
- recognize the types of paragraphs (main paragraph or thesis, support or argument, summary) and their functions
- list the main points of designated paragraph
- select a summary statement for a series of paragraphs
- review summary statements in written texts, then write your own
- draw conclusions using relationships among ideas
- draw conclusions based upon prior knowledge

CSML-047: QUESTION-ANSWER RESPONSES (QARS)

Introduction

In 1984, a middle-grades classroom teacher-researcher named Taffy E. Raphael devised a way to help reading students more easily find answers to questions.

This commonly used comprehension structure, *Question-Answer Responses* (or Relationships) offers a conceptual framework for locating correct responses and interpreting and applying ideas.

In this section, we work on expanding the answer to the question, "Once you have identified a question, what are the three means of locating an answer in text?"

- right there (literal)
- look for it (interpretive)
- use your prior knowledge or experience (inference or application)

Instructional Activity

Why Do We Need to Know This?

You need to know this to read for understanding.

Literal level skills include following directions, recalling facts and dates, recognizing main ideas, restating the pattern, and time lines (order and sequence of events). Detail questions are literal only if the reader can recall the answer without drawing on past experience or inferring from information presented in the text.

To find the correct literal response, easy-to-find details are found right in the question. This really is "reading on the lines." Right there" questions begin with the words: list, where, what is, when, how many, name, etc. The correct response is usually very short, one or two words.

1. **Read the following text.**

   QARs offer a conceptual framework for locating correct responses and interpreting and applying ideas. The original QARs are:
   o   Right there (literal)
   o   Look for it (interpretive)
   o   Use your prior knowledge or experience (inference or application)

2. **Respond to this question.**

   What are three methods for locating correct responses to questions?

   The correct answer is: Right there (literal), Look for it (interpretive), and Use your prior knowledge or experience (inference or application). In this case, the answer is found literally and exactly, in the text that was just read.

Interpretive answers are found by "reading between the lines." Although not directly there (in the text), the response is found by putting the author's clues together. Called "think and search," the reader searches for information throughout the passage or selection that applies and puts the ideas together to construct the most correct answer.

Words indicating the question requiring an interpretive answer are *include, summarize, retell, explain,* etc. The interpretive level stresses the relationship between the author's and the student's own ideas.

1. **Read the following text (more advanced skill level students).**
   One of the things a driver of an American car should know is that it has four ground-effect rims and tires, each of which is attached a wheel plate by either four or five nuts, depending on the make of the car. These are referred to as "lug nuts."

2. **Respond to this question.**
   How many lug nuts are used on the average American car?

   In this case, the author assumes the reader has the mathematical experience to multiply the number of lug nuts per wheel by the number of wheels. The correct answer is: Either sixteen or twenty, depending on the make of the car.

Finally, look for "on my own" types of questions that use what is already known to make an inferential or application response. This relies upon the student's background knowledge and opinions and is not, therefore, as text-dependent. It is, in effect, the best educated guess based on the known information presented.

In the application or inference level, which is one conceptual level higher than interpretation, a previously learned concept is applied and utilized. This is called "Transfer of Learning" or (from the instructor or coach's point of view) "Teaching for Transfer."

- **Read the following text and then respond to the question (more advanced students).**
  The American flag, like many other aspects of our country, has been allowed to change over the years. The first truly national flag carried thirteen alternating

red-and-white stripes with thirteen white stars on a blue field in the upper-left quarter of the flag body. Originally, both the stripes and stars were there to represent the thirteen states formed by the thirteen colonies. As the country has grown, the number of stripes has remained the same, but the number of stars has grown and still continues to represent the number of states."

- **Respond to this question.**

   How many stars were on the flag in the year 2000?

   The correct answer is fifty. In this case, the assumption for the right answer comes from previous knowledge that no new states have been added since the 1950s when Alaska and Hawaii were admitted to the Union.

Summary

Look for each type of QAR in various written materials. Start with easy text and progress to more difficult (and challenging) reading materials. QARs can be extremely valuable skills if they are reviewed and practiced at each progressive learning level and across every level of content.

Use QARs starting at about the third-grade level. At earlier skill levels, we recommend staying with the literal (right there) responses, possibly starting to make interpretations at about second-grade level. It is not a good idea to frustrate younger, emerging students or second language learners with inferential questions until they are ready.

CSML-048: FLUENCY AND RATE BUILDING

Reading Skills and Comprehension

Introduction

This is one of our favorite—but unbelievably neglected—mini lessons. In public schools, this is a very big deal and a significant factor in high-stakes testing. But not many teachers know the background of the mechanical aspects of teaching fluency and building rate. It does not just happen. Therefore, you are about to learn *Easy-Start* tried and true ways to build *automaticity*.

Automaticity means the ability to read accurately and quickly to get meaning from print. Some reading "experts" regard fluency only as the absence of word recognition problems. This is why it is called *automaticity*. Your student, as a fluent reader, must read smoothly, in phrases, with ease and a lot of expression. Certain words have emphasis. In the schoolhouse, students are tested on fluency. They must read a certain amount of words a minute, with accuracy. This is very stressful for kids but is done routinely. If reading is flat, expressionless, and "boring," fluency is lacking. This is usually caused when the words are unknown or your student is just not confident, stressed, or short circuited on basic word study. Then you need to revisit the basic fundamentals in word recognition. (The diagnostic-prescriptive-evaluative cycle is "teach, re-teach or proceed"). The more fluent the student, the better the comprehension. Word-by-word reading or stopping to break apart unknown words results in lost meaning.

The "good" reader matches reading skills, purpose, and rate to read fluently. Intonation, phrasing, and emotion—whether reading aloud or silently—are also important. Improvement in the physical aspects, such as rate, rhythm, shortening time of each "eye stop," and increasing the width of vision span per eye stop are all necessary to boost fluency.

Students who read one word at a time are focusing on letters. Fluent readers recognize whole words, phrases, or even (at advanced levels) sentences, all of which increase reading speed (rate) and comprehension.

Fluency development begins with flexibility of purpose. It then moves toward focusing on the mechanical. Way back in 1879, a French researcher named Javal noticed that a student's eyes don't move smoothly along a line of print; instead, they make a number of starts and stops per line. These are called "saccadic movements." Although the stops last only one-fourth to one-half of a second, these pauses are real and are easily noticed.

You can observe your student reading with these eye stops, simply watch the eyes move along the line of print and notice the number of stops per line. Your goal is to lengthen the span and lessen the number of stops. Encourage more rapid reading by first quickening the fixation and then widening the visual span.

At the same time, work to eliminate *back-skipping* (regression) as this both slows the reading rate and hurts comprehension. One possible method to accomplish this is using a metronome or lightly tapping a pencil to set a rate/rhythm of reading—and gradually increase the rate. This activity can be especially effective when working with both tactile-kinesthetic and musical-dominant learners.

If a student labors with reading, has trouble tracking the print, makes continuous errors, reads one syllable at a time or one word at a time, fluency should become the top priority! This plodding reading may be caused by a number of things, but usually it means the student does not automatically recognize new words. Fill in the gaps by going back to the first mini lessons on word study. Reading with lots of sounding out, following punctuation, and proper phrasing makes a difference.

In this mini lesson, we work with two major learning elements:

- expanding reading skills, rate, comprehension, and fluency
- building rate to boost fluency

Instructional Activity

Learning Elements

- **Echo Reading**
  Working at the instructional level, model oral reading for the student, reading slightly louder and staying just a bit ahead with the student also reading orally, slightly behind. As fluency develops, allow yourself to fall slightly behind the student, providing virtually instant correction to missed words or mispronunciations.

- **Repeated Readings**
  Prominent reading educators suggest this easy and excellent fluency builder. At the beginning of each practice session, have the student reread the same passage of approximately 150–180 words, working toward repeating it three times in two-minute increments. Each time, due to the concept of "overlearning," reading rate, fluency, and comprehension are enhanced. Record or graph the results. The National Reading Panel strongly endorsed this practice for numerous learning levels.

- **Start with Easier Reading**
  Since comprehension is one of the end goals of fluency, start with easy and familiar reading materials, increasing reading levels gradually to ensure the frustration level is avoided.

- **Use Recorded Books**
  Make recorded books, read-alongs, or recordings of the student's reading. Recorded readings definitely benefit

fluency, possibly because they fully engage three of the five senses.

- **Practice Oral Reading Daily**
  Take turns reading aloud with your student.
- **Practice Oral and Silent Reading**
  Repeated exposure to familiar words boosts fluency.
- **Retelling**
  While this practice is a comprehension builder, it also builds reading rate and fluency. It can be applied from small chunks (two or three paragraphs) to an entire section, chapter, or story. In essence, it accomplishes validation of comprehension of the material read and provides a foundation for subsequent reading.

  In *retelling*, students are asked to restate or retell the most important information and their reactions to the text or story. By building this framework, a student gets used to reading quickly to master the gist of the sentence, passage, or page.
- **Familiarity with Proper Phrasing**
  Provide a written selection,| telling the student to insert vertical lines between words | to highlight proper phrasing. Then read the passage(s) aloud, concentrating on the phrasing. Use of color coding works well.

Building Rate to Boost Fluency

Good readers approach different materials with flexibility. This means they alter their reading rate according to their purpose for reading the particular selection. As familiarity expands, so does speed. When unfamiliar with the material, either in content or skills, it is necessary to slow down.

Give skimming and scanning special attention. In both cases, the intent is to avoid reading one word at a time. The only reading method generally slower than this is *sub-vocalization,* reading out loud to yourself.

The greatest problem with reading speed in sub-vocalization is reading one word at a time, under the breath, which slows down the reading.

When surveying material by skimming, give special attention to headings, first and last sentences, etc. Let your eyes run down the middle of the page to gain an overview, stopping once or twice on a line. Another method is to focus on the white spaces between the lines rather than on the lines themselves. This is called subliminal reading or reading for concept (reading between the lines) to let the mind, rather than your eyes, gather information in larger chunks.

Scanning is slightly different. A page is scanned to pick out a specific fact or piece of information. One helpful technique is referred to as the crisscross method. Scan from the top-right corner to the bottom left, then glance at the top left and scan to the bottom right of the page. These advanced techniques reflect a higher level of fluency. But this gives you something to aim for as you move toward speed-reading, the topic of another book beyond the scope of this mini lesson on *Easy-Start* fluency and rate building.

Have fun teaching and learning with these surefire, research-based, classroom-tested methods. You are the deciding factor in your student's academic success!

The KWLW Wall Chart

K	W	L	W
Before Reading What do I already know?	Before Reading What do I want to know?	After Reading What have I Learned?	After Reading What would I like to learn next?

Figure 48-1: KWLW Wall Chart

CSML-049: RESPONDING TO LITERATURE

The Writing Connection

Introduction

While the major focus of this series is language structures and reading processes, we need to understand that every part of writing is important as well. From basic print conventions to the writing process itself, each reading mini lesson in this series is accompanied by a writing component. There are a multitude of excellent instructional titles that deal with how to teach composition, but here are the fundamentals:

We work with two major learning elements in this section:

- basic steps in the process of writing
- ideas for combining reading and writing

Sharing is the most important part of the writing process. Reading to a partner for positive feedback helps polish the finished product. Writers write for readers to read; writing encourages the writer and reader to share a common understanding. We write for an audience. So what we write—and how we write it—matters.

Prerequisites for Learning

Reading and writing are closely aligned in the study of any language. Symbolic writing begins early, but writing to share information requires a more advanced knowledge of language structures and basic grammar. The student understands that letters make words, words form sentences, and sentences are made up of several different classes of words.

Most of these concepts are reviewed within this section, but students must be able to read and understand the language on at least an emergent level.

Why Do We Need to Know This?

Reading Champs considers *writing* the final of the four legs on the workhorse we call language. These legs are the four sequential steps to becoming a capable communicator. The first is *listening*, the second is *speaking*, the third is *reading,* and the fourth is *writing.*

Of course, without writing, there can be no readers! Through writing, we share thoughts, memories, concepts, and knowledge. Writing can be interpreted, copied, and edited, but the actual original words, once written and published, are permanent. Writing—offering relevant thoughts in an organized manner—is the way for people to recall the past, record the present, and influence the future.

Learning Activities

Here are a few good ideas for combining reading with writing:

- keep a reading journal
- do "quick writes" on a daily basis, starting with one minute (from the time you decide on a subject) and working up to ten
- respond to reading through writing at every opportunity
- edit and check the spelling of all written work
- master new vocabulary and immerse it in your daily life
- experiment with a variety of online, book, magazine, and report formats

- review and practice outlining processes
- write in a variety of genres
- avoid worksheets, fill-in-the-blank, scrambled words, word searches, and nonsense words assignments
- always find and use appropriate models
- review the writing processes and use them constantly and consistently

Language Structures

Parts of Speech/Sentence Usage

Language is made up of thousands of words and phrases. The English language is made up of nine parts of speech that define the function of the word (or phrase). The parts of speech are:

- *Nouns:* A noun is the name of a person, place, thing, or an idea or concept. Nouns within a sentence are often signaled by an *article.*
- *Pronouns:* A pronoun is a word used in the place of a noun. Usually, the pronoun is a substitute for a specific noun, known as its *antecedent.*
- *Verbs:* A verb is a word which, when used in a sentence, expresses action (*action verbs*) or a state of being (sometimes referred to as *be verbs.*).
- *Adjectives:* An adjective is a word used to modify, or describe, a noun or pronoun.
- *Articles:* Sometimes classed as adjectives, articles are used to mark nouns. There are two indefinite articles (*a* and *an*) and only one definite article (*the*).
- *Adverbs:* An adverb is a word used to modify a verb, an adjective, or another adverb. It usually answers one of the following questions: *When? Where? How? Under what conditions? To what degree? Why?*
- *Prepositions:* A preposition is a word placed before a noun or pronoun to form a phrase modifying or describing another word

in the sentence. The prepositional phrase usually functions as an adjective or an adverb.

- *Conjunctions:* Conjunctions join words, phrases, or clauses to indicate the relationship between the joined elements.
- *Interjections:* Interjections are words (usually single words) used to express surprise or emotion. (*Wow! Hey! Oh!*) But they can also appear as phrases.

Source: A Writer's Reference
Diana Hacker
Bedford Books of St. Martin's Press

Helpful Hint for Learners

Every sentence must have at least a noun and a verb, but there are one-word sentences where the noun is "understood" by its context without actually being spoken.

Eight Basic Steps in the Writing Process

1. *Prewriting*: In this first step, which provides the foundation for writing, the writer (student) completes a fast write or free-flow of ideas for a specific period of time. This may include using a graphic organizer, such as an outline or web, for organizing ideas. If you are "stuck" getting started writing, put on some quiet music, set a timer, and say, "Let's just write whatever you think about the subject for three (or five) minutes." It may take several brainstorming sessions to get the ideas flowing. Refer to KWLW in Mini Lesson CSML-039.

2. *Rough draft*: This second step focuses on content and organization. Many writers do much of their work in this stage on a two-column page to facilitate addition or restructuring of the manuscript as the final step in this part of the process.

3. *First revision*: The third step is the first revision done to correct initial obvious errors in spelling or grammar and to encourage logical flow. The main goal is to make it clear for the reader and avoid anything obviously off-topic. Revising content and editing are crucial; since processing writing is a loop, encourage your

budding writer to do as many drafts as necessary until the final work is accurate and readable.

4. *Editing*: The fourth step is to read the manuscript thoroughly, looking for remaining grammar and spelling errors as well as tense and conjugation problems. Correct anything that does not follow the logical flow you have planned for the story.

5. *Second revision*: In the fifth step, we finish all the corrections identified in the previous edit. Now, as we write, we are looking for subject-verb agreement and other verb problems, pronoun-antecedent agreement, double negatives, fragmented sentences, and punctuation errors. Most students think that something has to be perfect on the first draft, but professionals believe it is best to let the piece "breathe" a little before going back and doing another revision or two.

6. *Final edit*: Best practice, time permitting, is to set a final draft aside for anywhere from a day to a week and then read it again from beginning to end. Look for incorrect or imprecise language, words used too often, appropriate and consistent flow of language, excess or unnecessary words, avoidance of run-on sentences, and proper punctuation.

7. *Final revision*: In this step, the focus is on format. Manuscripts should be double-spaced on one side of standard-sized (8-1/2" by 11") paper. Place identifying information in the upper left-hand corner of the page. The ideal type style for a manuscript is 12-point Helvetica or Times Roman with margins 1-1/4 inch all around. Handwritten items should be neat and clean without scratch-outs (which usually means you will be copying from your final draft) and should be written with at least a line height between lines.

8. *Publishing*: Everything is done except getting your work out to readers. In the case of a student, this is not much of a problem.

Additional Learning Activities

A great deal of the process of learning to write is reading the kinds of well-written materials (stories, papers, books, etc.) that are focused on your topic and genre. Essentially, this says that it is unlikely you will ever learn to be a good writer by watching television, playing video games, or reading comic books.

The best thing you can do to become an outstanding championship writer is read! Read often, read with depth, and technically engage yourself in the text instead of the story. Why did the author choose to describe this event the way he did? How do the choice of words and the structure of the text affect you, and why? Can you feel the author's interest and the passion, and does that affect the way you view the subject?

You, as a student or a coach, should also be aware of the six analytic writing traits, including:

- ideas and content
- organization
- voice
- word choice
- sentence fluency
- conventions

The first five of these traits usually come under revision. The sixth, conventions (spelling, capitalization, punctuation, grammar and usage, and paragraphing) fit in the editing process.

Summary

Effective writing must be clear, organized, well supported, and filled with detail. It must have an engaging voice—the writer's passion for the subject encourages lively, expressive writing. Sentences that flow together and fit well with conventions of grammar and usage make the work easy to follow. Finally, precise, clear language provides a vivid, easy-to-follow picture between author and reader.

Sharing is the most important part of the writing process. Reading to a partner for positive feedback throughout the process helps polish the finished product. Writers write their works for readers to read; process writing encourages the writer and reader to share a commitment to excellence!

And by the way, this book has been edited and revised more than two dozen times prior to being released for publication.

EPILOGUE

Steffen's Story
Teaching a "Left Behind" Child to Read

October 2004

When Rita Wirtz came into our lives, my son's school career was in jeopardy. This was not the result of any lack of motivation of effort on his part. Basically, Steffen had been labeled as ADD. This, however, was in contradiction to the comments from teachers, coaches, tutors, and friends who noticed how "brilliant" Steffen was. To say I was confused and uncertain about where to find help is an understatement.

Rita was recommended to me by one of her college students who was tutoring Steffen. She recognized that Steffen's learning challenges were out of the scope of her experience. After meeting with Rita for the first time, I immediately knew she was an answer to my prayers, indeed, a miracle.

My son began two-hour sessions, once a week, with Rita in January of 2004. At that time, he was in jeopardy of failing. He was barely at first-grade level halfway through the second grade. Rita poured her energies and expertise into my son's learning challenges. After a few sessions, Rita did what the pediatricians, optometrist, Title I reading specialist, and teachers could not accomplish. She figured out how to teach Steffen to read and write.

Steffen ended his second grade nearing grade level. He improved in every subject and behaviorally. He now has the confidence to be in third grade. He now loves to read! He now loves school. The mystery was solved.

In closing, no words can express my gratitude, admiration, and respect for this woman and her dedication to children. She is not kidding when she says, "No child left behind!" Thanks to Rita, Steffen won't be left behind.

Sincerely,

Margot Delfino
Steffen's proud mother

Steffen's Story
Where Is Steffen Now?

January 2014

Steffen is seventeen years old, a high school senior. He is in the top 5 percent of his class of approximately four hundred students. His GPA over the last four years ranges between a 3.94 and a 4.0 in advanced placement classes. He is involved in many school organizations, is cocaptain of the speech and debate team, and has placed twentieth in the entire state of California in his division of Student Congress. Steffen has absolutely no problem speaking in public or having a conversation with some of the most educated people around. He is an avid reader and loves to read and write.

At this time, Steffen is in the process of applying to the top universities and service academies to continue his education and has with a high interest in the science fields. Steffen is a confident, loving, caring young man. He gives a lot of his free time to various charities without being asked.

In 2004, before he was introduced to Rita Wirtz, if I was told this is where Steffen would be today, I may have questioned you. He has come a long way from the little boy who cried every morning, saying, "I hate school. I don't want to go today." He is excited about going to a top college.

I shudder to think what could have happened to Steffen if he did not learn to read and was not taught how to overcome his reading challenges. What if I had not found Rita who lovingly but with a strong determination found how to teach Steffen to read, spell, and write?

In my opinion, the public school system in 2004 was leaving Steffen behind. When Steffen was placed in a "special" reading class in the first grade, he said, "Mom, I know how to speak English. I don't know how to read!"

My husband, Jeff, who came into Steffen's life when he was three years old, encouraged me to get Steffen help. Like me, he knew we had a very smart boy on our hands who was being overlooked and falling through the cracks. This is when we took matters into our own hands. We knew we had to find Steffen the right help and quickly. When we found Rita, Steffen's life changed.

Steffen, Jeff, and I will forever be grateful for our Angel, Rita. We only hope her teachings will help many other gifted children who may be left behind or help just the average child to read and not fall behind.

Margot Delfino-Gavar
Steffen's very proud mom!

AFTERWORD

I believe that one dedicated person can make a difference. I started teaching when I was about six years old, playing school at home with the neighborhood kids. My mother and father really pushed education. We read together, shared *Reader's Digest* vocabulary boosters, and played Scrabble and other word games. My mother volunteered for adult education. I started going with her when I was about thirteen years old, and I knew for sure that I was going to be a reading teacher.

After I completed college, my teaching career began in junior and senior high school classes. I was teaching middle school English and reading and high school speech, drama, and reading lab. I was already worried that my students couldn't read very well. It was the start of my lifelong journey into the field of reading. In the forty years since then, I have enjoyed a truly interesting and remarkable career.

I have been a classroom teacher, reading specialist, and site principal. I have worked in several state and local education offices, taught college and university teacher-training courses, and been a keynote speaker and seminar presenter across the country, No matter what I was doing, I was, first and foremost, a reading teacher.

I'm an old-fashioned grandma. I live in a historic home in the mountains of Northern California. In this creaky old house, I have taught about thirty underachieving students. For a while, I had an interesting experience teaching Native American children of the Miwok Tribe.

Once, when I was giving free parent reading lessons at the independent bookstore in a nearby community, my husband and I met a family of rodeo performers. Their kids were named Rider and Roper, but Rider roped and Roper rode. We invited them to dinner in our home, and I gave the boys reading lessons by the fireplace.

Rather than focusing on me, I'd like to share a few special memories of some kids I met along the way. It is amazing to see what our children can accomplish. Here are just a few of the thousands who left footprints on my heart.

Jessica, Ninth Grade

(Dad writes) Hi, Rita. Last spring Jessica was tested at a 4.2 grade reading level. This week she was tested again. Now a 9.8 reading level!

Nick, Tenth Grade

(Mom writes) Hi, Rita. I just wanted you to know that Nick got four As on his last report card. He is doing really well. He also qualified for the ski team.

Alec, Third Grade (Bilingual)

Dear Mrs. Wirtz. Thank you for coming to our classroom. You taught us blends and digraphs. We had fun. I learned so much from you.

Caroline, Eighth Grade (Bilingual)

Dear Mrs. Wirtz. Thank you for taking the time to help us be better readers. I enjoyed all the reading, study, and eye exercises. I will remember to do these exercises so I can be a better reader.

I wrote this book because it needed to be written! After years of mandated curriculum, reading scores have a very long way to go. There is little statistical educational growth. When only about a third of our children are proficient readers and writers, we're in big trouble!

Every day, I believe I become a better teacher. I understand the way children learn. For many years, I studied brain research, learning styles, and multiple intelligences. I can honestly say there are many things I don't know much about, but I truly know how to teach reading. My greatest joy is sharing my life's work with others. Now I am both proud and humbled to have the opportunity to share a lifetime of experience with you.

The bottom line is that our children deserve the best. The latest national test scores in the United States confirm what most educators already know—very few of our kids can read at or above grade level. *Reading Champs* shares patterns and systematic sequences that can help parents, tutors, reading coaches, and professional teachers achieve the lofty goals behind the common core curriculum standards.

Reading programs come and go, but skills remain forever!

Mrs. Rita M. Wirtz, MA
Parent, teacher, and creator of *Reading Champs*

BIBLIOGRAPHY

Common Core State Standards Systems Implementation

For more information, visit these California Department of Education Websites:

Common Core State Standards (CCSS)
http://www.cde.ca.gov/re/cc/
Curriculum Frameworks
2013 Revision of the Mathematics Framework
http://www.cde.ca.gov/ci/ma/cf/index.asp
2014 Revision of the English Language Arts/English Language Development Framework
http://www.cde.ca.gov/ci/rl/cf/index.asp
Supplemental Instructional Materials Review
http://www.cde.ca.gov/ci/cr/cf/suptsupmatreview.asp
Professional Learning Modules
http://www.cde.ca.gov/re/cc/ccssplm.asp
English Language Development Standards
http://www.cde.ca.gov/sp/el/er/eldstandards.asp
Smarter Balanced Assessment Consortium
http://www.cde.ca.gov/ta/tg/sa/smarterbalanced.asp
Career Technical Education Model Curriculum Standards
http://www.cde.ca.gov/ci/ct/sf/ctemcstandards.asp
Next Generation Science Standards

Time-Tested Reading Resources for
Parents, Teachers, and Coaches

** = *Limited Availability*

Adams, Marilyn Jager. *Beginning To Read: Thinking and Learning About Print.* MIT Press/Center for the Study of Reading. Urbana: University of Illinois, 1990.

Bialostok, Steven. *Raising Readers, Helping Your Child in Literacy.* Winnipeg, MB: Penguin Publishers, Limited, 1992. **

Farstrup, Alan and Jay Samuels. *What Research Has To Say About Reading Instruction.* International Reading Association, 2002.

Iverson, Sandra. *A Blueprint for Literacy Success: Building a Foundation for Beginning Readers and Writers.* Bothell, WA: Wright Group, 1997.

McCracken, Marlene J., and Robert A. McCracken. *Reading, Writing, and Language: A Practical Guide for Primary Teachers.* Winnipeg, MB: Penguin Publishers, Limited, 1979. **

McGuiness, Diane. *Why Our Children Can't Read and What We Can Do About It.* New York: Simon and Schuster, 1997.

Routman, Regie. *Literacy at the Crossroads.* Portsmouth, NH: Heinemann Publishers, 1996.

Tarasoff, Mary. *Reading Instruction That Makes Sense.* Victoria, BC: Active Learning Institute, 1997.

Moustafa, Margaret. *Beyond Traditional Phonics, Research Discoveries, and Reading Instruction.* Portsmouth, NH: Heinemann Publishers, 1997.

Neuman, Pressley and other editors. *Best Practices in Literacy Instruction.* New York: Guilford Press, 1999.

Mrs. Words' Favorites

Amberg, Jay. *The Study Skills Handbook*. Good Year Books, 1993.

Armstrong, Thomas. *The Myth of the ADD Child*. Penguin, 1995.

Booth, David, ed. *Literacy Techniques for Successful Readers and Writers*. Pembroke Publishers, 1996.

Bromley, K., Linda DeVitis, and Marcia Modlo. *50 Graphic Organizers for Reading, Writing & More*. Scholastic.

Carbo, Marie, Rita Dunn, and Kenneth Dunn. *Teaching Children to Read Through Their Individual Learning Styles*. Allyn and Bacon 1991.

Cipriano, Jeri S. *Dynamite Dictionary Skills (Good Apple)*. 1997.

Davis, Beth, and Bonnie Lass. *Elementary Reading Strategies That Work*. Allyn and Bacon.

Davis, Donald D. *The Gift of Dyslexia*. Ability Workshop Press, 1994.

Dodge, Judith. *The Study Skills Handbook (Grades 4–8)*. Scholastic Professional Books, 1994.

Fountas, Irene. *Guided Reading: Good First Teaching for All Children*. Heinemann Publishers, Portsmouth, New Hampshire, 1996.

Fry, Edward and Jacqueline Kress. *The Reading Teacher's Book of Lists*. Prentice Hall, 1993.

Grammar Works! (Grades 4-8) (Reproducible Skills Lessons). Scholastic, 1996.

Mangrum, Charles, Patricia Januzzi, and Stephen Strichart. *Teaching Study Skills and Strategies in Grades 4–8*. Allyn and Bacon, 1998.

Miller, Wilma. *Reading and Writing Remediation Kit.* Center for Applied Research in Education, 1997.

Muschla, Gary. *Reading Workshop Survival Kit.* Center for Applied Research in Education, 1997.

Pavlak, Stephen. *Informal Tests for Diagnosing Specific Problems.* A. Parker Publishing Company, 1983.

Pinnell, Gay and Irene Fontis. *Word Matters.* Heinemann Publishers, Portsmouth, New Hampshire, 1998.

Stowe, Cynthia M. *Spelling Smart! A Ready-to-Use Activities Program for Children with Spelling Difficulties.* Center for Applied Research in Education, 1996.

Weaver, Constance. *Teaching Grammar in Context.* Boyton Cook Publishing, 1996.

Other Great Literacy Titles

Billmeyer, Rachel and Barton, Mary Lee. *Teaching Reading in the Content Area.* McREL, 1998.

Isaacson, Marlys. *Picture Me Reading.* 2002.

Morrow, Lesley Mandel and Linda B. Gambrell and others. *Best Practices in Literacy Instruction.* Guilford Press, 1999.

Weaver, Constance, ed. *Practicing What We Know (Informed Reading Instruction).* National Council Teachers of English, 1998.

ABOUT THE AUTHOR

They call her Mrs. Words. *She walks the talk!* Rita Wirtz, an acclaimed teacher's coach, classroom teaching dynamo, and reading specialist and consultant, received standing ovations and rave reviews wherever she appeared.

A sought-after keynote speaker and motivational performer, Mrs. Wirtz presented her Reading Champions! Easy-Start Reading workshops across the United States. She also worked for several national seminar companies, offering teachers "The Very Best Classroom-Perfected Reading Strategies Ever!"

Mrs. Wirtz, parent of four, taught language arts, English, speech, and reading at every skill level, preschool through adult, including lab, clinic, and classroom for more than forty years. She also worked as K–6 and preschool principal, and at both county office and state department levels. Positions included curriculum consultant, literacy trainer, and Title I reading program evaluator.

With her vast practical experience and love of children, she really knows what works to teach all students to read or read better and faster. She is especially expert with underachieving children having reading challenges.

For many years, Rita taught reading courses for several universities and mentored a multitude of credential and student teachers. In addition, she taught school administration. Most significantly, she made weekly "house calls" to schools, modeling reading strategies demonstration lessons in nearly six hundred K–12 classrooms. Rita routinely taught fundamental reading skills to learning diverse students.

Mrs. Wirtz trained reading professionals, teachers, administrators, school board members, teaching assistants, parents, and tutors across the country. She keynoted for the California Department of Education, university commencements, and organizations such as Mentor Teachers, Early Childhood Education, Learning Disabilities groups, Special Education Program Specialists, Migrant Education/Mini Corps, Bilingual, Child Welfare and Attendance, etc.

Rita currently volunteer teaches, makes warmhearted special appearances, and writes. She lives in her historic home built in 1858 on seven acres in the Sierra Nevada Mountains. She enjoys her barn, a pond, a big poodle named Gus, geese, deer, and other wildlife, not to mention scores of visiting family, friends, and children.

Experience for yourself why thousands have flocked to Rita to catch her spirit and feel the joy of teaching students to be capable, confident readers. Most importantly, children of all ages become Reading Champs!

Reading Champs offers common sense, practical strategies. She teaches you the essentials of reading instruction, including shortcuts, interventions, and corrective strategies, for kids who don't get it the first time around. Experience the best research-based, classroom-proven strategies that instruct word understanding, vocabulary, comprehension, and fluency. Now *you* can make the difference.

Rita's academic background includes a BA in English and speech, a reading specialist certification, a master's degree in reading, and an administrative services credential.